OKLAHOMA Zen

THE PHILOSOPHY OF THE CIMARRON KID

Roger Hudiburg

Drawings and cover painting drawn by Roger Hudiburg

Interior Design:
Concepts Unlimited
www.ConceptsUnlimitedInc.com

Boulder, CO

WARNING: This book is not political or religious but may be controversial to many, radical to some and heresy to a few.

ISBN-13: 978-0-61590-241-8   (pbk)
ISBN-10: 0615902413

13   14   15   16   17   0 9 8 7 6 5 4 3 2 1

First Printing, 2013
Printed in the United States of America

DEDICATION

To William T. Bozarth, Jr.:

Bill, ya taught me to question everything and we always had a good time.

—The Cimarron Kid

To my wife, Peggie, my friends and family:

Thanks for all your encouragement, love and assistance.

—Roger Hudiburg

Roger Hudiburg

A NOTE
FROM THE CIMARRON KID

Just in case someone's interested, I give my permission to Roger Hudiburg to write-up this here philosophy of mine—my own special way of dealing with life. He'll probably be more fancy and windy than I would, but I'm too lazy to write it myself. I expect he'll do a good job. If he doesn't, I'll kick his ass; in a non-violent way of course.

Hudi's gonna tell you somethin' about me, I guess, but I just want to say some things about myself before he gets started. Although a lot of Oklahoma Zen has always been with me, I have changed some over the years. Oklahoma Zen has caused a lot of those changes. I thought you ought to know about it.

I used to be a cowboy, but I really wasn't. Then, I was a beatnik, but I really wasn't. I was also a mountain man, but again, I really wasn't. Now I'm a husband and a father and that's for real!

I am also a spaceman—you'll have to read the book to figure out the meanin' of that.

I've quit my rough and rowdy ways and I don't hunt or fish no more. I still pick the "geetar" but I don't perform as much. I share the housework with my wife and we spend a lot of time walkin' and talkin'. I've been cuttin' my lifestyle down to the "bare bones" and I'm right proud of it. I got a long ways to go but I'm gettin' there and Oklahoma Zen sure ain't hurtin' me none in the process.

Just one more thing. I want you to know that I thought the title of this book should be: "*The Essence and Dissonance of the Naked Raga*" or "*The East Met the West and Was Summarily Pared to the Bone.*" Hudi disagreed with me, sayin', "That sounds too intellectual and snobbish." Hell! I worked on that title a long time; it's anything but frivolous! It's got art in there, and music, and it's the "meat" of Oklahoma Zen. I wrote a piece of guitar music about ten or fifteen years ago and gave it the same title. It says the same thing this book does. It's not snobbish, I just like words. And a good joke.

Well, see ya on the river,

The Kid

TABLE OF CONTENTS

PROLOGUE

"What is the matter with the East,"
said the Beast,
to the Boy?
"What's the matter with the East,"
said the Boy,
"is there ain't no joy!"

"The matter with the West,"
the Clown confessed,
"is too many shoes,
the Ten O'clock News,
and too many bucks!"

"And, the crux...
of what is the matter with the West,
keepin' a'breast!"

Prologue
WHO THE HELL IS THE CIMARRON KID?

The Cimarron Kid wrote the poem on the opposite page.

The Cimarron Kid also made-up Oklahoma Zen.

All his life he has been searching; searching for answers to the philosopher's perennial questions, "Whence I come, whither I goest?" and "How do I keep on truckin' with the most efficiency and the least pain?" He has looked and he has found some answers that work for him. This book concerns those answers and represents a balanced blend of teachings and methods that constitute a recipe for joyous and meaningful life.

Where did the Kid look for answers? He left many stones unturned in his quest because he is by nature a lazy fellow. He has paid his dues, however, for he has searched in places many people have ignored or not noticed. He has also invested a significant amount of time and energy in this search. He was always directed by his two goals in life, increase of love and knowledge.

The Cimarron Kid drew his answers from a variety of sources; the variety being intentional as well as natural. The sources are experiential as well as academic and include life and work experiences, literature, art, music, family, friends, teachers, etc. We all have learned from these kinds of sources but because of the variety of his sources, their inclusion and utilization in his own evolution and their synthesis into a simple, harmonious system, I feel that he has something valuable to share with others.

The Kid has consciously and constantly pursued this knowledge. He has, throughout life, purposely forced himself into new situations and forced situations onto himself that would help him learn and would challenge him to apply what he had already learned. As he learned new things, he altered his life accordingly when this new knowledge helped him achieve his goals. By utilizing what worked and discarding what didn't, he developed the system he calls Oklahoma Zen, hereinafter referred to as OZ.

I don't want to bore the reader with a complete list of all the sources of knowledge that the Cimarron Kid has explored, but I do feel the necessity to offer a sampling of these resources. It is important to establish his credentials and to explain at the outset why OZ is unique enough and practical enough to justify the time it takes to put it all down and then to read, study and practice it.

The Kid has been very lucky to have had a wide variety of experiences and adventures. These include such things as learning camping, survival and other wilderness skills at a very early age. Roaming the woods, floating the rivers, hunting, trapping, fishing and just basically "playing Indian" offered experiences from which anyone could learn and profit and apply to all areas of life. He hitchhiked all over Oklahoma while very young, making a longer trip to the Okefenokee Swamp in southern Georgia at the age of seventeen, carrying a poncho, jungle hammock and one change of clothing (see song later in this introduction based on this adventure). He has worked as a lifeguard, cook, janitor, carpenter, farmhand, singer, musician and teacher. He has taught swimming, lifesaving, guitar, banjo, first aid, wilderness/survival skills, yoga, chess and archery. As a public school teacher for twenty-two years, he has taught science and mathematics. Though raised a Christian, he has studied religion from atheism to Sufism. As a student of athletics and fitness, he has concerned himself with such diverse activities as football and Tai Chi Chuan. He has participated in political and environmental organizations and has also been fiercely independent. All these experiences and many others helped to formulate OZ.

Literature has always been an important part of the Cimarron Kid's life. He read mostly science fiction and adventure stories during his teens, but was also exposed to beat poetry and literature and the classics. As his life continued, he found more and more joy and knowledge in expanding his literary interests to include everything from metaphysics to physics, from the Bible to Henry Miller, from Homer to Mickey Spillane, from Robert Ardrey and Robert Rourk to Ken Kesey and Tom Robbins and from Gurdjieff to Gibran. His university studies (B.S. in Geology and M.N.S. in Education) of course helped round out his reading skills and resources but he seems to cherish most those books and other pieces of written work that he ferrets out on his own. I'll never forget the day he discovered Rabelais'

Gargantua and Pantagruel in the library at Oklahoma State University!

Art has constantly been a focus in the Kid's life, both for growth and for enjoyment. He has played and sung for thirty years as a folk musician. His music has often been a "ticket" into areas and events which would otherwise be off-limits. Drawing with pencil, pen and brush has sporadically interested him since he was very young. As the reader will notice, this book is illustrated with some of his pen and ink drawings.

As in other areas of experience, music has always been an eclectic pursuit for the Cimarron Kid and a rich treasure-field of probable answers to life's questions. His interests and activities span Grande Ole Opry to Grand Opera, hillbilly to classical. I have heard him perform his music for a variety of audiences and he has always presented a mixed-bag of selections that are both educational and entertaining.

With most of his interests, the Kid has followed and advocated a "do-it-yourself" philosophy. He has written some of his own music and I have included examples in this book. One such song follows and is a chronicle of the hitchhiking trip mentioned above:

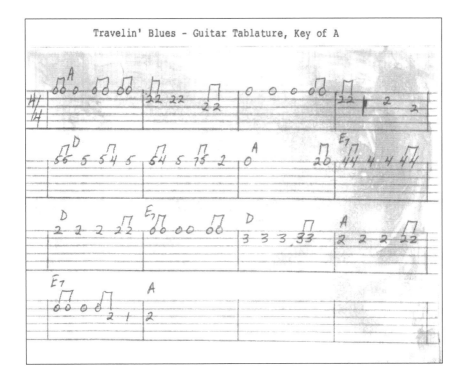

Travelin' Blues - Guitar Tablature, Key of A

Travelin' Blues,
The Cimarron Kid (1969)

Gather 'round boys I'll tell you a tale.
About the time I rode on the southern rail.
Rode her all over this beautiful, bountiful land.
I was a rippin' along on a southern coast.
Just a roarin' along on a southern ghost,
I got the travelin' blues and I got to be gettin' along.
A train whistle blows off in the night.
A diesel truck roars on out of sight.
It's cold outside but I'm as warm as the sun.
I bought a cup of coffee with my last dime.
But I can make more money any old time,
I got the travelin' blues and I got to be movin' on.

My old buddy he turns to me,
And he says, "My friend, it's great to be free.
We slept last night underneath a railroad track.
We bathed in the river and we washed our face.
We live a fast life, but we live our own pace.
We got the travelin' blues and we got to be gettin' back."

On Jacksonville Beach in Sherman Park,
In Waycross, Georgia til way after dark,
We roared around and out to the ragin' sea.
On Clarksville Ridge, doin' what we please,
In Okemah town livin' a life of ease,
We slept in the shade of a grand old pecan tree.

Now I'm tellin' you boys it ain't all cream.
This bummin' around ain't always a dream.
Of the last ten miles, I must have walked eighteen.
But, it's a real grand feelin' at the end of the line.
With an old guitar and a jug of wine,
This bummin' around beats anything, I've seen.

It seems unnecessary to mention the influence of friends, family and various teachers, ordinary and esoteric, on the formulation of OZ. However, I can't deny the importance of contact with other people in helping the Cimarron Kid see things more clearly, helping him change his mind and approach, reinforcing ideas, methods and concepts and exposing him to new ideas, methods and concepts. I only wish I could name everyone with whom the Kid brushed minds, psyches and bodies during his long search and many journeys. He has told me that he feels very fortunate because of all of these relationships and wishes to take this opportunity to thank everyone for their friendship and their help.

Who the hell then is the Cimarron Kid? Why, he's my best friend and he's asked me to write this all up for him.

Roger Hudiburg
Boulder, Colorado 1983

Prologue

WHAT THE HELL IS OKLAHOMA ZEN?

The OZ is a method which can be used to accomplish certain goals that we may set for ourselves. The Cimarron Kid uses OZ to expand and increase his love and knowledge in all their various forms. It is a comprehensive, harmonious system that combines teachings from the East and the West. It allows the "twain to meet." It is highly individualized so that each practitioner may decide the extent of OZ in their lifestyle for goal-realization. However, it is also a fully-balanced and total package that is original to OZ and critical to its practice.

OZ takes from the East such concepts as nonviolence, simplicity, awareness and the oneness of all things and mixes them with the practicality, common sense, joy and rugged individualism of the West. In addition, certain earmarks of the East, like ego-reduction and management, have been included in OZ and balanced with Western counterparts such as the "good-ole-boy" attitudes and lifestyles of places like Texas and Oklahoma. There are many other attributes of both the East and West that are part and parcel of OZ but these will be brought out in the following chapters. The six methods that constitute OZ are given as follows and will be the chapter headings for this book:

The Six Methods of Oklahoma Zen
1. Awareness
2. Simplicity
3. Non-Aggression
4. Growth
5. Service
6. Joy

OZ is very simple and straightforward. Therefore, this book will be presented in the same manner. It will be carefully edited so that all extraneous and repetitive items are omitted and, by the way, painfully operated upon to remove as much ego-inflating material as the Kid can stand—this is done in the spirit of Oklahoma Zen!

OZ is not a religion! It does include certain values that are held in common with many of the world's religions, the Golden Rule being a good example. It also achieves, in my opinion, a very high morality in that it speaks for the sacredness of not only all life but of the entire universe and all it contains and expresses the need for man to assume the role of caretaker and help maintain and nurture all things. However, OZ is not a religion because it does not require belief in a supreme being and it does not require adherence to its methods for eternal salvation, attaining Nirvana or dissipation of bad Karma. A follower of OZ can believe in anything they care to and still be faithful to its methods. The methods are used only to help people realize their goals.

OZ is also not a political system! It is true that parts of OZ seem to postulate a certain economic system which could be confused with politics (by following the methods of OZ a person would tend to be less a consumer and less a producer of material goods). However, the Cimarron Kid thinks of this non-materialistic approach to life as not an economics system but something that transcends economics or at least relegates it to a subservient rather than a dictatorial position. A person could study and follow OZ and continue to participate in the politics of their choice. OZ is concerned with individual and not collective revolutions.

OZ is a philosophy, according to the Kid's way of thinking. OZ advises the reader how precisely to act, to live, to grow, to learn, to love and to interact with your environment and with other people. OZ gives detailed directions, exercises and methods to use to achieve certain goals. It is easy to explain and to list the methods but very difficult to put into practice. That corollary to Murphy's Law, "There is no such thing as a free lunch," certainly applies here. However, if a student decides to work at all, then as much success can be achieved in reaching self-set goals as energy is expended. Input = output!

Even though this book is not religious or political, it may be considered dangerous by some for the following reason. If a number of people, especially people in positions of leadership and influence, altered their life in the direction of simplicity, non-aggression, awareness, joy, etc., then this could radically alter the direction of mankind. Such time-honored institutions as war, the industrial/military complex, organized crime, planned obsolescence, economic and political systems, organized religion, and the medical and legal professions might decline in need and popularity. This might force a lot of folks out of a job and require re-training to re-enter the work force. This is dangerous to these people and institutions. It boggles the mind!

Now, of course, any reasonable reader knows that this book is not going to seriously affect enough people to disrupt the present world situation, so there's nothing to worry about. Nothing at all!

What the hell then is OZ. It is what it is! The Kid refuses to pin it down any more than what I have said above. Read on if you want further definition.

The book will contain six chapters, one for each method of OZ and an Appendix on how to apply OZ and use it properly in everyday life. Each method will be defined and explained from the perspective of the Cimarron Kid. Following this, input from the East and West will be detailed. Then, the subject will be discussed according to certain basic human needs and diversions such as health, relationships, shelter, work and play.

Since OZ promises to be comprehensive, I am trying to cover as much ground as possible. However, OZ also demands simplicity. Each chapter will therefore attempt a concise sampling and fine balance of the profound and the mundane, the serious and the frivolous, the heavy and the light necessities and escapes of mankind.

Indian Song - Guitar Tablature, Key of A

Chapter 1
AWARENESS

I am sleeping, here in the valley.

I am sleeping, down here below.

I am sleeping, here in the valley.

But I won't sleep for lo-o-ong.

Til I awake.

I am a mother, I am a father.

I am a sister and brother too.

I am a baby, an innocent baby.

I am part of everyone,

E-even you.

I am the mountain, I am the ocean.

I am the prairies, forests so green.

I am the glacier,' I am the desert.

I am the rolling wa-a-ter.

So sweet and clean.

I am a lily, growing in my valley.

I am an oak tree, I am the seed.

Yes, I am the acorn, a wildwood flower.

I am a mountain columbine,

I am a weed;

I am a chipmunk, I am the grizzly.

I am a carcass, rotting on the ground.

I am a vulture, I am a bluebird.

And, I fly around, around, around.

And, around and around.

I am the Buffalo, the Passenger

    Pigeon.

I am the Dodo, Tyrannosaurus Rex.

I am the Whooping Crane, I am the

    Eagle.

I fly around, around, around,.

Who will I be next?

I am sleeping, here in the valley.

I am sleeping, down here below.

I am sleeping, here in the valley.

But I won't sleep for lo-o-ong,

Til I awake.

Indian Song

The Cimarron Kid

1968

Someone once explained the difference between men and other animals by saying, "All animals think but only man is aware of his thinking." The Cimarron Kid's explanation of awareness is similar. When we speak of awareness in this book we mean not only paying attention but watching ourself paying attention. This includes paying attention to all our selves: our physical self, our intellectual self, our emotional self, our sexual self and even our intuitional self. We must also constantly observe the interaction of all these selves with each other, with the selves of others and with our total environment.

This has been described by the psychologist, philosopher and teacher Gurdjieff as "self-remembering." Alan Watts said to "sit quietly and listen" in order to learn who you are and what is your place in the universe. Artists, athletes and scholars come close to our idea, of awareness when they point out how important it is to concentrate on their goals and techniques. It is the kind of awareness that allows us to shoot an arrow from a bow naturally, to play tennis or golf without conscious thought and all the negative emotions that go with that, to fix and ride a motorcycle with a sense of well-being or to cook a loaf of bread so that you feel a part of the process.

The awareness we're defining here is decidedly Eastern in flavor. Oh, I know that in the West we talk about awareness: "If you kids would just pay attention you would remember that the homework was due today!; "Why can't you be more sensitive to my feelings?"; "Don't leave my tools out in the rain!"; "You forgot our anniversary!"; "I just ran a red light, officer? I musta spaced it out." But in the East they literally make a religion out of it. It is a part of OZ that definitely borrows from the East and it is meant here to be applied on the cosmic scale that is envisioned in the East. However, the OZ person must be of their time and place—they cannot go hide in some monastery and dream about reality; they've got to live reality. Input from the West makes it necessary to avoid an easy route of meditatively sitting in the lotus position, amidst the soothing sounds of tinkling bells and trickling water, learning to be aware in an environment free from distractions. We must develop awareness in spite of distractions if we are to have the balanced, total approach to life that the Kid insists on.

We have all experienced moments of heightened awareness; those moments when certain smells, sounds, visions, feelings and tastes seem to vibrate with reality and are etched in our consciousness seemingly forever. How often does an odd memory drift into our thoughts at the strangest times? I'll bet these pieces of the past hearken back to times of intense awareness. Most of these moments are accidental. The trick, according to the Kid, is to make them more conscious, natural and more frequent.

What would it be like if all men and women were more aware? What if we all paid more attention to our environment, to our elders, our spouses, our children, our friends, our teachers and our pupils and last but not least, to ourselves? What if you were more aware? What if **you** were totally aware?

Gurdjieff said that most people go through life

asleep—sleep being the antithesis of awareness. He also said sleep causes accidents and is the primary sin of mankind. All our troubles: war, crime, pollution, over-population, greed, famine, poverty, alienation, loneliness, cruelty, poor health, etc. are related to unawareness. He added to this that one hundred "truly awake" people could significantly change the world. The Kid believes this to be true. So do I.

Increased awareness reduces accidents. Accidents cause suffering. Therefore, increased awareness reduces suffering. Reducing the number of accidents seems to be a huge benefit from which we can all profit. The benefits are easily recognizable and instantly obtained when greater awareness is applied to any and all parts of life.

For a trivial example let's take a man's shaving ritual for each morning of his life. When you don't pay attention when you shave you are likely to hurry and scrape, burn and cut your face. This causes discomfort and is time-consuming (time to care for the nicks and to worry about them). It also will involve a certain amount of self-deprecation—"You Idiot! How could you be so careless and stupid?" This might even escalate into a spilled or broken after-shave bottle or, horrors, the razor knocked off the shelf into the toilet! It has happened, believe me. I speak with authority on the subject. This could dictate the man's attitude and affect his approach and techniques in dealing with the rest of the day. It is obvious that being more aware could help out our hypothetical shaver. It is not so obvious that all our lives are cram-packed with incidents like this, so much so that it's a wonder that we survive at all.

What about the lady who, unaware that it requires so much time to get ready for work, is running late and rushes out to her car spilling the second cup of coffee from her favorite coffee mug on her favorite slacks in the process? Cursing herself for not allowing more time, she places the mug on top of the car (thinking, as she does so, that she better not forget it) as she searches her purse for her car keys. You know the rest of the story, don't you? It's happened to all of us in one way or another. She drives off with the mug bouncing off the back of the car to break into a hundred pieces on the cement of the driveway. If she's more aware than most of us she will remember the mug about now. Otherwise, she will drive on to think of it later; probably at a very inopportune time.

Here's an example of better awareness and its consequent benefits that the Kid told me specifically to include at this time. He said he tried to quit smoking for years but was unable to do so. He attempted to quit for all the good reasons; the common reasons we hear so frequently. It's a dirty habit. Or, it's unhealthy. It burns holes in your clothing and furniture. It's expensive. None of these excellent arguments for quitting seemed to be adequate to do the trick. It was not until the Kid sat down and made the effort to be totally aware of his situation that he realized the reasons for quitting weren't as persuasive as his main reason for continuing. The awareness of this primary motivation for his smoking was shocking and painful to admit. He discovered that his smoking was done to help the "Marlboro Man" image, the macho, outdoorsy look. He'd been completely sucked in by Madison Avenue. When the Kid decided he could be a "man" without the cigarettes, cigars, chew and pipe, he easily kicked the habit. He says, "Without really watchin' myself I wouldn't a known that and it wouldn't a stuck for the last fifteen years. I don't know why other people use tobacco but I know that's why I did and that's a stupid reason for doin' anything."

It is no accident that the first method of OZ is awareness. Improved awareness is the single, most important change a person can make in their life. To illustrate this on a more important scale than the above examples, I choose the concept of the Golden Rule.

Religion is the primary tool of man to promote good behavior. One essential ingredient in all the world's great religions is the Golden Rule or some variation thereof. The practice of the Golden Rule cannot exist without awareness and the more aware we are the more we can realize the potential inherent in this great teaching. How can we treat others as we ourselves wish to be treated unless we are conscious of our own and other people's needs? When we judge whether someone is "good" or "bad" we frequently concern ourselves with how they treated their fellow man. With increased awareness we will treat each other better and also increase the common good. As the Kid would say, "Now that's better than gettin' stuck in the eye with a sharp stick."

Now, let's see what OZ has to say about awareness as it applies to specific needs and diversions of man and woman.

The Cimarron Kid once had a discussion with a "survivalist" concerning what were the important things to plan for in the event of a nuclear attack or some other disaster. The survivalist went through the usual list of food, medicine, water, tools, weapons, clothing, sleeping bags and so forth. He also mentioned an easily-defendable place to hide it all in. The Kid said, "Good health and marketable skills are the most important. If ya got those, everything else will fall into place. If ya don't have 'em then your ass is grass cause no matter how many goods you store up, you're still vulnerable. Nobody'11 steal your health or skills. Hell, if you're real careful, nobody'll even notice ya got 'em."

Awareness can help you maintain your health. Paying attention to your physical, emotional and intellectual needs will not only help you to survive but to do so with a high degree of quality. Many of us are not as aware of our health needs as we are the latest football scores or fashion forecasts. Our ears perk up when the car knocks so we fix it ourselves or we rush it in to the mechanic. But, if our body knocks, or our mind squeaks or our thought processes get rusty, we seldom notice it until it's too late. Or worse yet, some of us are aware of pressing health problems but do nothing to help ourselves. In the OZ system, this is just another facet of unawareness.

Awareness, as it pertains to our health, means sorting through all the false alarms that we receive from our egos, mass media and other various advisors. The powerful persuasion we get from all of these sources is not always meant to deceive us, in fact it's usually given with the best intentions. It's just that it usually applies to a hypothetical, generalized human being or a laboratory rat. Nobody knows us like ourselves, if we are truly aware. The Kid says, "When I quit smoking, I did it because I wanted to, not because the Surgeon General said I had to." We must learn to listen to ourselves in order to make the best diagnosis of our needs and the best plans to follow toward better health. The biggest villain in all this is our own ego. Our ego, for example, tells us to exercise to look better. Our inner sense tells us to exercise to feel better and better looks are just icing on the cake.

Nutrition is a familiar subject that underlines the need to be cautious with the expert's advice. People continually eat and drink things they don't like and that don't fit in with their balanced needs at all just because some magazine or friend told them to. Sometimes, this just makes us miserable. At other times, it can be downright harmful. Just because something like vegetarianism or, on the other hand, refined sugar, is proclaimed as good nutrition by various food gurus, is no reason that it is necessarily good for you or me. Our own nutritional needs have to be determined by us according to our special situation and then conscious choices have to be made for our own proper diet from the plethora of food alternatives available today. Our total, balanced diet has to be part of our awareness. Our diet has to conform to emotional and intellectual needs as well as physical.

OZ says we must strive to improve our awareness of our health and then act on this knowledge. OZ also says that the balance mentioned above has to extend to all our other needs and diversions as well. Getting complicated? As the Cimarron Kid says, "This is about as easy as threadin' cooked spaghetti through a wild pig's nose. But nobody ever got anything done by standin' around thinkin' about it. Get after it! Time's a wastin'!"

OZ health awareness includes paying attention to all parts of our selves constantly (this is meant literally). You're sitting in a meeting and you become aware of several sets of muscles that are tensed from stress. You notice this and relax them, realizing that the tension serves no purpose. Or, you suddenly realize that you have been speaking too fast and too loudly. You slow and quiet yourself. Someone is talking but you're not listening. You make the effort necessary to stop whatever fantasy you're spinning in your head and concentrate on the business at hand. You have a habit of clearing your throat all the time, or grinding your teeth, or tapping your fingers or your feet. You get angry at people and inanimate objects for all the wrong reasons and suppress appropriate anger or misdirect it. Be aware of what you're doing and how it harms your body, mind and soul and then work on yourself toward balanced and better health. As mentioned before, special exercises, skills and techniques to put the six methods of OZ into practice will be listed and explained in the Appendix.

Our relationships with other people are also very important to work on in terms of awareness. There is so much potential for love and for knowledge in our dealings with others. This speaks to the Cimarron Kid's goals of increased love and knowledge. Whatever your goals may be, you will have a better chance to realize them if you are more aware. Of course, there is a huge capacity for adversity as well. How much of our misery, our loneliness and disappointments our neuroses and psychoses, our ignorance and hate stems from how we treat one another? And how much of these negative emotions are born from accidents due to unawareness? We've already spoken of the Golden Rule and how awareness helps in our struggles to get along with each other. Imagine with me for a moment the tremendous surge of positive energy that would develop if we could be more aware of what our parents, children, spouses, friends and colleagues care about, what they're afraid of, what they love and hate, what they want and don't want out of life, and yes, even their presence. What a tragedy for friends, strangers and even enemies to be ignored. A tragedy for them and for us.

The tidal wave of love and knowledge that would develop from increased awareness in personal relationships just might be one thing that could fight the entropy of the world of physics; the heat death of the universe. The glorious energy of human love and the organizational powers of the human mind, unleashed and exponentially-growing, just might overcome chaos. R. Buckminster Fuller, the great designer and builder of material and human architecture, the inventor of the geodesic dome, said as much in his writings. Many others have spoken of the wonders and powers of love and knowledge, but they are practically useless without awareness; the keen, unrelenting, ubiquitous awareness that OZ demands.

The Kid knows of what he speaks when he mentions the powerful need of children to be noticed. I've already

told you about his twenty-two years of teaching experience in public education. He says,

When parents ask me for help in understanding and controlling their kids, I always tell
them to pay more attention to their children.
It sounds real simple but it is hard as hell to
do. It's hard to understand and even harder to
put into practice.

I see little tykes and teenagers just beggin' for
their parent's or anyone else's awareness.
You've got to stop what you're doin' and listen
and act. And then, most importantly, follow
through! Damn, I see so many parents tell
their kids, "Now stop that, you hear me!", and
then without watchin' to see the results, they
go right back to their newspaper or soap opera
or whatever. The child, who's smarter 'en hell
about all this, waits until dad or mom does
their thing, and then they go right back to their
thing. Sometimes the parents couldn't see or
hear their kids if they were ten-ton Mack
trucks bearin' right down on 'em. Now, let me
tell ya Hudi, all this applies just as much to
every other relationship on this planet. Shit
fire! Most of the time we're blind as bats, and
about some of the most important stuff there
is.

OZ encourages awareness in all our dealings with other people. Fortunately, the art of paying attention to one person is uniform in its application to all our relationships. If you learn to be more conscious of your children's needs, then it is an easy step to use this skill in working and playing with all others. So, listen to and watch other people and your reactions to them and try to improve yourself. Any small change will produce beneficial results and this can develop into a chain reaction. Love is catching! You'll be a model for others to follow. The Kid believes that this is what Christ meant by "turning the other cheek."

It is necessary to mention at this time that none of OZ can be practiced in just one or two areas alone. It has to be a total, comprehensive effort. Awareness involved with relationships must fit hand-in-glove with awareness in all other areas.

Another need that we have is shelter. We must protect ourselves, make ourselves comfortable and ensure our privacy. A home and clothing that pleases us aesthetically are also important because art and beauty are every bit as much a requirement as utilitarian demands. However, when we don't pay attention to ourselves we frequently get carried away with things. The old ego rears its ugly head again. OZ awareness, as it refers to our home and garments, dictates that we do what we want but we make sure it's inner-directed and not outer. We learn to resist "keeping up with the Jones." When we are bombarded with a steady stream of seductive advertising, we become more discerning and selective. We don't avoid television, magazines, billboards, newspapers, etc. like some would have us do, we just teach ourselves to know "in our bones" what really fits us and our goals and face all the other stimuli with benign indifference.

The Cimarron Kid once told me that he always wanted a pool table; lusted after it until he finally bought one. Friends and relatives tried to tell him that it wouldn't be long until the new wore off and then it would become a stone around his neck. Sure enough, after a few weeks of being a joyous companion, the table became a tyrant and the Kid found himself, instead of playing pool because he really wanted to, doing it solely to justify the purchase.

> That damn table was as useless as the third verse in a church hymn. I finally sold it to a good-ole-buddy. He still has it cause it fits his needs. It didn't fit mine. If I'd of been more aware I'd a known that I was just givin' in to outside pressures and not listenin' to that little-ole-me that dwells within. At least I was aware enough to notice my error and to take care of it.

If people want to have their decisions made for them by designers and salesmen, then that's fine. If they are aware and act on that awareness, then that fits with OZ. Yes, even "clothes horses" can be OZ practitioners. The Kid is a far cry from this but he says, "Some of my best friends wear designer jeans and drive sports cars." Divergence from OZ occurs when people clothe themselves or surround themselves with paraphernalia that is totally determined by someone else who is self-appointed to the position of expert in one field or another. When people give themselves up blindly to their gurus, whatever the so-called experts are selling, then they are not aware in the OZ sense. The Kid hates this the most in the realm of organized religion, but I stray from my path.

If we listen to our inner voice, as concerns our needs for shelter, then we will not only be more comfortable with our surroundings but will be more in balance and in tune with the rest of our life. Much more will be said on this subject in the next chapter.

Awareness is necessary at work and at play also. We should strive to pay attention all the time even though we may only succeed one-millionth of the time. This is probably more than most people achieve and it will make our life better. When we play and watch games, work at our hobbies and our professions, when we indulge in entertainment, when we practice and observe art, we should watch ourselves carefully and consciously. When we laugh or cry, when we make love or war, when we are alone or with others, we should have more knowledge of what we are doing and why. We must ask, "What motivates us?" "What are the purposes and the results, the causes and effects?" And we should always be aware enough to act; to put into motion the plans we have made. I think it was Ayn Rand who said through one of her characters, that to "aim without moving and to move without aiming" was a terrible thing to do. OZ demands awareness of thought, feeling, action and consequences but above all else, action, and action without accident.

One thing that needs to be said at this time is that all this awareness can carry a terrible price with it if again we are not aware. We must recognize when to let loose of our seriousness and realize that we cannot solve all the problems we will notice with our increased awareness. We must know that there are times not to act, times to be detached, times to develop a "wastebasket" mentality to deal with all the trash—throw away that which we can't or shouldn't affect. This is sort of the other side of awareness but is still part of it. The Yin and Yang if you will. There are no opposites, just different parts of a continuum. If we are over-stimulated by our awareness, then stress and paranoia will set in. This reduces joy which is an equal part of OZ. Again, we must work for balance within, without and in between.

As the Kid would say, "Nuff said! Let's mosey on over to somethin' simpler." Therefore, we end this chapter in order to confront the second method in the OZ manifesto—simplicity, simplicity, simplicity....

The Wild Bird Cries Truth.

The Old Tree Preaches Wisdom.

—Zen Saying

The Wild Bird
Cries Truth
The Old Tree
Preaches Wisdom
—Zen Saying—

Chapter 2
SIMPLICITY

Talkin' Status Symbol Blues
The Cimarron Kid (1963)

Well, you ask me why I work so hard.
Gotta keep a Cadillac in my front yard,
A power boat in my garage.
And, a membership in the Country Club Lodge.
Got a electric toothbrush, electric vibrator chair,
    electric can opener
Supportin' the power trust.

I buy every one of them best sellin' books,
But, I don't read 'em, that's for kooks.
All I want to do is keep up with the Jones,
I got fifteen different colored telephones,
In all the rooms, in the closets, and in the garbage can.
And, that baby's chrome-plated.

Now, I watch television whenever I can,
Tryin' to be an educated man.
I buy every thing they tell me you see,
Why, I even bought me a color TV,
For my bathroom, can't afford it,
And, I'm goin' blind.

Now, I go to church about once a week,
But., it's not religion. that I seek.
I'm a good church-goer as everybody knows,
Just come here to show-off my new suit of clothes.
Who's that bum in the third pew, in the overalls,
Why, he's a prayin, just like the rest of us.

You know, there's some crazy guy lives down by me,
He don't even have a color TV,
No second car, no power boat.
Why, his wife don't even have a mink coat.
To. wear to church. He's a non-conformist, a beatnik,
A communist.

You know, doesn't look like he works very hard,
Just lays around in his back yard.
With a grin on his face that gives me the chills.
Why, he don't even have no unpaid bills,
Mortgages, revolving-charge accounts, stuff like that.
He's downright UNAMERICAN!

[Done in the Talking Blues style.]

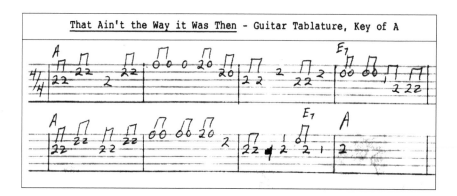

That Ain't the Way it Was Then
The Cimarron Kid (1968)

When I was a young lad I used to go swimmin',
In a dirty old river, well even with the wimmin'.
We took along some innertubes and we was all a grinnin'.
And, that was the way it was then.

Now, today all the kids when they go down to the swimmin' hole,
They take along a beach towel, shower clogs and radio,
Soda pop, candy bars and afterwards the picture show.
And, that ain't the way it was then.

We used to be content just to go down to the roller-rink,
And, watch the people go around, we even had time to think,
About what you're gonna do if a gal gives you the wink.
But, that ain't the way it is now.

Today all the kids have their own private TV sets,
Telephones in their rooms, they got lots of money, yet,
Let's don't blame the kids cause Daddy is a buyin' it.
And, that is the way it is now.

Today people have so much they don't know what to do with it.
They've got so much assorted junk they're havin' trouble storin' it.
Why, Sammy Smith has even bought a Handy-How-To-Store-It kit.
And, that is the way it is now.

There's snowmobiles, second cars and boats everywhere you look,
Campin' rigs with charcoal grills and four-burner stoves to cook,
Your dinner while you read your forty How-To-Fix-It books.
And, that ain't the way it was then. But, that is the way it is now.
So, give me the good old days.

The Kid's first OZ-type hero, Henry D. Thoreau, once said about the art of writing, "You must work very hard to write short sentences." Yes, it's very hard to be simple. Artists know this fact; the good ones anyway. So do scientists and statesmen; again the good ones. All people who have tried to achieve perfection in what they do and to derive maximum pleasure from their activities, sooner or later rub up against the concept of simplicity, how valuable it is and how difficult it is to achieve. We keep hearing things like, "The great lessons are simple ones," "Don't muddy up your designs or music with extra garbage," "Slow down and smell the flowers," or, "All my possessions and my social schedule seem to own me, to tyrannize and control me."

OZ simplicity borrows heavily from the East but is refined by Western traditions and perspectives. Simplicity in this book is not asceticism or austerity. It is not the loin cloth and spinning wheel of Gandhi nor the shaved head and rice bowl of the Buddhist monk. It is not eschewing material and emotional baggage but rather being consciously (awareness again) selective and discriminating in all that we do so that what we do carry is comfortable and functional and gives us pleasure instead of hassle. I guess the best way to state it succinctly is to call it "elegant simplicity." You will begin to see what I mean, shortly.

The Cimarron Kid uses the following formula when deciding between various alternative solutions to any given problem. "Hell, I just ask myself which solution is the simplest and which does the least harm. I just apply that when I have trouble makin' up my mind." (We'll speak to the nonaggressive portion of this formula in the next chapter.) All things considered, OZ holds with the idea that complication usually causes more problems than it solves.

The painter, Francisco Goya, regarded simplicity as an important part of his life and work. "I do not require much in the way of furniture for my house for I think that with a print of *Our Lady of Pilar*, a table, five chairs, a frying pan, a cask of wine and a guitar, a roasting spit and an oil lamp, all else is superfluous." He, obviously better aware of his own needs than anyone else, decided what was unnecessary for him and discarded it.

This isn't to say that OZ requires that we imitate Goya. Quite the contrary, we don't copy anyone, at least not exactly. We listen to our inner voice, and as Goya did, we summon up the courage and the necessary further awareness to act on what we hear. We should work for simplicity in our lives but the degree of simplicity will be different for all of us for the simple reason that we are not exactly alike, only similar, and some of us more similar than others. We imitate Goya and others only to the extent that we learn from their experiences and apply these lessons to ourselves but only as they fit inner-directions. I quote the Kid again on the subject, "It takes all kinds to make up the world. I'm glad I'm not one of 'em." The Kid also mentioned a geography professor that he knew from graduate school at Oklahoma University that described his conception of Hades as a place where everybody would look the same and talk the same as him (the professor).

As before, the idea of simplicity in the OZ system will

be clarified as we see how it applies to some specific needs and diversions that we all share.

Our physical health can profit greatly by simplification. The American public is becoming more health-conscious as is evident from all the latest diet and exercise fads and crazes. But, even though we are giving this need added priority, the very fact that each new fitness discovery is attended by all the hype and ballyhoo, all the glamour, pomp and ceremony of a Hollywood production or a coronation points out the need for simplification. It seems that we can't be fit without all the "how-to" books, appropriate, "fashionable" attire, proper terminology (practically a new language in some cases), terrible expenses, organized group activities and above all else, competition.

Witness the jogger. We'll start with the shoes; costing anywhere from $25 to hundreds of dollars. These must be stylish, comfortable, engineered for safety, chosen to satisfy the individual jogger's own requirements for terrain, tempo, physical ailments (Oh, Yes!) and peculiarities. Sometimes they have to have shock absorbent pads added and they often have accessories like a key and coin purse. These are just the shoes for God's sake! "Sounds like buyin' a car," says the Kid. Add to this a headband, shorts, shirt, wrist bands, socks, foul-weather gear, stereo tape machine with headphones, warm-up suit, subscription to *Runner's World* in hot, little fist, dues and organizational responsibilities for one or more runner's clubs, and entry fees for races and we're talking big bucks—you could conceivably spend $500 to thousands of dollars for all this clutter just to do what the Apache Indian used to do, seventy miles at-a-whack, with just a loin cloth and moccasins and a mouthful of water that they would sparingly drink during their race. And worse yet, this spells complexity with a capital C. All this junk has to be studied, purchased, used, cleaned, stored, maintained and fussed over. Then, of course, it wears or goes out of style, so you start all over.

To add insult to injury (sometimes literal as well as figurative) the jogger is often involved in something else in the fitness realm like bicycling, racquetball, cross-country skiing, tennis, or hiking and we have a whole new list of complications. Ouch! The first thing you know, you've sacrificed any health gains by becoming more and more, just another over-stressed rat in the proverbial race.

"Keep it simple," says OZ. Choose the best exercises for yourself but keep them in balance with everything else. How much of the accoutrements and entanglements for our fitness games come from outer-directed demands and from ego-satisfaction? Make sure that what you do to exercise your body is really what **you** want and need. Then, after you've analyzed the situation, "go for it" within the bounds of **your total** abilities and goals. Again, whatever you do must be harmonious with other health needs and with all the rest of your total person.

As concerns our diet, it definitely pays to keep it simple. We eat too much, too fast, too often and too fancy. All of these negative factors are partly encouraged by the lack of simplicity in our diet. Raw vegetables, nuts and fruits are simpler than cooked and are better for you. This holds true if they are also uncanned, unspiced and unsugared. High fiber foods are simpler, both in production and preparation than fatty meat and refined products and again better for you. Consider all the complications that arise with the incredible array of packaging, additives, storage, transportation, marketing, advertising, etc. that is common with most of our food products of today.

If we follow this argument to the extreme with our diet we would all be natural, organic vegetarians in the strictest sense and we would probably all be healthier physically. There is a problem here, though—this would be ver-r-ry boring to most of us. In applying simplicity this fanatically to our diets we would be forgetting the balance necessary to a true practice of OZ. If we are going to increase the love for ourselves and others (again, the Kid's goals) then we have to keep in mind other requirements such as the need for adventure and variety that most of us share. Our emotional health is inextricably entwined with our physical self and all the rest of our selves and must get its due attention.

The idea of "elegant simplicity" is very prominent here. If we simplify too much then we reduce the amount of joy (see Chapter 6) in our life and thus we are out of balance. This brings us again to the very essence of OZ; that we must apply all methods simultaneously and diligently but according to our self-determined needs and goals. Nobody promised that this was going to be easy. The Cimarron Kid describes it in this manner:

It's like three people ridin' a log down the river. One guy is the brain, the second is called the heart and the third is the body. The log is the ego. If they don't balance, they fall off and everybody's all wet. Ya also got the current and sandbars, rocks, old junk cars, snappin' turtles, alligator gar, and water moccasins to mess with. Add to that, the feistiness of that ole log, bein' all twisted and unbalanced and all, and ya got real problems. Ha! Just like in real life. If you don't do your balancin' act ya get eaten up. If ya keep it simple, it's easier.

What happens to our emotions when things get too complex? We usually break down in one way or another. It goes almost without saying that we should keep our emotional self on a simple and thus healthy plane but everywhere there is evidence that this advice is unheeded. This is especially true with negative emotions. Gurdjieff said we should learn to not express negative emotions. The Kid believes that what he meant by non-expression of negative emotions is not the usual technique of suppressing said emotions but to teach ourselves to not even express them internally—in other words, to just not have negative emotions in the first place. Now, it is a huge understatement to say that this is difficult to do, but OZ simplicity can help us here.

Through the practice of OZ we can learn to be more aware of our negative emotions. Then, we can study what is causing us to react in the way we do. At attempt should be made to learn to not react as much to the given stimulus that is bothering us. This involves simplicity in that we isolate our problems and act on them one at a time and in so acting, work to make our responses less complex and less irritating.

An example might be a situation where we are trying to tell a story or explain something and something is constantly interrupting us. We should be aware of our reactions to these interruptions and pay attention to what they are doing to us in a negative way. If we find the irritation and our responses intolerable, then we should immediately work to simplify things. One method is to decide that whatever we were saying probably wasn't that important anyway so we just sort of allow our conversation to taper off and strive to remain quiet and just listen for a while. Learning to talk less and listen more is OZ simplicity at its best.

But, suppose that we can't seem to muster the necessary resources to slow and quiet our reactions? Then, an additional simplification would be to break off the conversation abruptly on one pretext or another and simply detach oneself physically from the troublesome situation. In the future we should try to avoid the situation or the person that causes the situation to develop. As you can see, this calls for more awareness and simplicity. The bugaboo here is our own ego. We must be aware enough, strong enough and willing enough to cut through all the crap and act on our needs to make our life less complex.

One thing that complicates just about everything in our lives is speed—trying to do more and more, faster and faster. Gandhi said, "There is more to life than increasing its speed." Speed, for the sake of speed, is non-productive, causes accidents and stress and is contrary to all the methods of OZ. It is a form of aggression (see Chapter 3) against ourselves and others. It is especially opposed to simplicity. The Cimarron Kid told me a story about a time when he learned a great lesson about speed and its negative aspects.

He was in the Bahamas, in Freeport, riding in a cab. With him in the taxi was an elderly, black Bahamian; immaculately but very comfortably dressed, leaning on an ornate walking stick with both hands clasped, one over the other, on the gold-inlaid head of the cane. The old gentleman seemed to be very cool and relaxed despite the heat, very calm and contented. The cab driver asked if his passengers would mind if he took the time to drive a little out of the way to pick up another fare. The Kid shrugged and then the old man said slowly but firmly and with a heavy accent, "Life is too sweet to hurry." The Kid said to me, "That has always stuck with me, Hudi, and when I started makin' up Oklahoma Zen, I knew that slowin' down had to be in there somewhere. If everybody would just make it a point to find some lil' ole thing to slow down each day, I gar-an-tee that they'd notice positive changes right away."

One of the biggest problems man faces is to organize the information that comes his way. All our intellectual processes tend toward complexity it seems, so our intellectual health is definitely an area that needs simplicity desperately. I'm reminded of a story concerning the psychoanalyst, Fritz Perls. It seems he had listened patiently to a long discourse, amply peppered with fifty-dollar scientific terms and intellectualeese, about the various illnesses with which a particular mental patient was afflicted. After the long-winded explanation, he sat for a minute or two contemplating what had been said and offered this summary: "What you mean is that the poor bastard is scared." This is the kind of simplicity that OZ strives for where intellectual matters are concerned.

Think about the endless, boring meetings many of us have to attend. Think of our propensity for "dragging things out," for repetition, for "making our point," for exaggerating the importance of so many issues. Pay attention to how much of this is really meant to meet the objectives of the meeting and how much is to feed our own ego. It seems we have to constantly make sure everyone knows, what we know, because it's **so important**. If we could just make an effort to simplify what we think and say at meetings alone, what a service we would do for ourselves and our fellow human beings.

Think about how we always have to name things, photograph things, categorize things, systematize things, even when we're doing something supposedly as simple as taking a walk in the woods. Be aware of how complications get between us and life. Remember how our intellectual-self dictates our life with ever-increasing complication. One of the Kid's pet peeves is some people's over-indulgence in 'picture-takin'." He recognizes the art and beauty in photography and enjoys looking at family albums, vacation slides and movies and nature photographs as well as the next man, but he has some very caustic remarks for those that get too carried away with all this, especially when they get in his way:

Gawd-al-mighty! Have ya ever seen some of these characters loaded down and clankin' around with all this crap hangin' all over 'em—two or three cameras, extra lenses, range-finders, light meter and on and on, tryin' to climb a mountain or float a river? They spend all their time haulin' and worryin' over their equipment; that is when they're not takin' pictures. They don't seem to take time to see nature without somethin' in between them and the object of their attention. And, everything's always in the way, like when they try to climb through a bobwire fence. Hell fire, everything does a flip/flop, the pictures and the picture-makin' become a reality and the rest of the world is all in the imagination.

Now, I'm not talkin' about the ole boy or ole girl who does this for art, or his work, or to pre-serve a few memories. I'm talkin' about the person who seems to need to live in the past all the time or needs to blot out the bad stuff he sees all around him or needs to build some kind of a 'rep' for theirself; they make picture-takin the end-all of everything and do every-thing in their power to suck you into their act. I sound mad, but I really just pity them cause their life is so complicated by their so-called hobby that they're missin' all the real stuff.

Damn, I do go on, don't I? Of course, what bothers me doesn't make much difference anyway. Everybody's got to find their own level. I'm just tryin' to show how some people can get their lives all cluttered up and they don't even know it. I used to be the same way with my huntin' and fishin'. That's one of the reasons I quit.

Our personal relationships too often suffer from lack of simplicity. Sometimes we have too many relationships, at other times the relationships are just too complicated and still there are instances where it is our total social schedule that's overloaded. Most of us have reached that point from time to time when we exclaim. "I wish all my social obligations would just vanish. My life is so tied up and controlled by other people and events that I just can't stand it any more!" By using the idea of elegant simplicity we can reduce those frustrations and maybe abolish them altogether.

OZ would tell us to deepen rather than broaden our friendships. Keep it simple! Decide which friends and relatives, which social and family gatherings, which business acquaintances and colleagues mean the most to us, which give us the most joy and which help us the most in reaching our goals. Then prioritize and concentrate on the top of the list. In order to simplify, we must also systematize.

After we systematize, we must stick to the system. This seems to be the hardest part for many people. Learning to make yes and no decisions based on previously worked out programs, to make them immediately and consistently is a very difficult thing to do. This especially holds true when you are working as a team, husband and wife for instance. OZ demands that we do this increasingly in all parts of our lives, and that we do it consciously and in balance with all other methods of OZ.

A good example that the Kid mentions in this context is Christmas card lists. These lists tend to get more complicated year after year. If we feel that it is important to send Christmas cards, then we should do so using a system that works toward making them shorter and more pertinent rather than the opposite. The worst thing we can do in an OZ sense, is to keep sending cards to someone with whom we don't want to continue a relationship just because they always send us a card. We would be doing everybody a favor to discontinue this practice swiftly and surely.

Sexual relationships, as we all know, can be very complex. One of the biggest problems, according to the Cimarron Kid, is mixing sex up with just about every other part of our lives. The sex force is very powerful and will take over practically every part of our existence if we allow this to happen. It also gets constantly misdirected. The Kid, says, "If it ain't natural, it's unnatural." He also has a good friend who is fond of saying, "Too much sex is almost enough." If we could only learn to add a little simplicity to our sex lives we might not be so frantic and fractured in other areas of our lives.

There are many, many ways OZ can be applied to our sexual behavior. The basic thing we can say here is we think too much about sex and do too little about it. Instead of fantasizing so much and building up tremendous pressure that is relieved oftentimes in miserable ways, we should simply have sex when we physically crave it. This of course, only has validity when it is in balance with the rest of OZ. So, it must be done with awareness, nonaggression, service, growth and joy. In other words, we shouldn't worry so much about time, place, performance, appearance, game-playing, ego, etc. We should just let it happen.

This doesn't mean that we should drop our pants whenever the urge hits us in the drug store or on the bus. Custom, morality, pregnancy, legality, taboos and many other restrictions apply here. If we violate one or more of these, then we also violate OZ if only because we are just complicating matters again. What is being said here is that we can and should simplify our love life by letting nature take its course without so much of our constant intellectual and emotional intervention. Let's have sex "while the coffee pot boils over"; with responsibility but without so much mental chatter; with meditation, without intellectualizing; with joy, without ego. Let's make love with our bodies more and with our minds less.

We should also be aware of how sexual energy complicates our lives when we misuse it through violence, aggression, competition, narcissism, ego-enhancement, social-climbing, career-enhancement or as a means of providing ourselves with money and material goods. How much better our lives would be if we applied the idea of elegant simplicity to our love life by removing these negative factors. There will be more discussion of misuse of sexual energy in the next chapter—Nonaggression.

Simplicity can be applied more easily under the headings of shelter, material goods, work and play. Also, the benefits are more immediate and easier to perceive. I will explain what the Kid thinks are good examples in each of these areas. With this explanation, the reader will quickly be able to think of many more ideas. Whether he or she agrees with these applications of OZ is of course another matter.

The Cimarron Kid has for a long time felt that Western architecture and design could stand some simplification and still retain elegance, beauty and comfort. For instance, why do we build huge houses, in excess of 2,000 square feet, for a standard family of four and then fill them up to the brim with furniture, utensils, bric-a-brac and decoration? Why not build smaller homes and have fewer accessories? We could still have the same living space. Instead of massive furniture and room dividers and walls, possibly pillows and screens in the oriental fashion? Rather than a dozen reproductions of paintings, why not one or two originals? There is something startlingly beautiful about a wall with one picture or a table with one vase, especially if the picture and vase are unique and arranged properly and if they have good artistic quality. They are also easier to care for and clean, and the total expense and worry is less. Elegant simplicity!

The Kid has never lived in a home with a garage. When asked why, he repeats the OZ *Law of Space and*

Junk: "The more space ya have, the more junk." And, I guess he is right. Have you ever noticed how most garages are so full that the cars are rarely parked inside? One way to simplify your life is to get rid of storage space or at least don't build any more.

Let's address the space surrounding our homes. If a person really enjoys gardening and working in the yard, then it makes sense to landscape intricately and profusely. However, many times I have heard people "bitch and moan" about how their yards tyrannize them, making them work all the time. If they are sincere about this, then OZ would advise them to cull, remove and reduce, to use more low-maintenance and natural plantings, to have smaller yards and to learn to appreciate dandelions and other weeds.

I must include here an example from my own experience. One of the debts I owe to OZ is my release from slavery to collections. I'll mention a couple of them here. I used to be in love with books and records. Not just reading and listening, I still do a lot of that, but collecting them, amassing large quantities of them and then lining them up on more and more shelf space so that they were quite visible to me and to visitors to my home. I categorized them, dusted them, rearranged them, moved them, felt of them, memorized their titles and so on. After studying OZ for a while, I began to realize that the main purpose for my having so many books and records was ego-oriented; I wanted to make a big show of my interests. There was no way I could possibly read or listen to them all, in fact the sheer preponderance of numbers precluded my enjoyment of my favorites, or at least interfered with it. So, I began giving them away. What freedom I experienced! What joy in subduing my ego and simplifying my life. It also felt good because the large fractions of my collections that I gave to friends, libraries and book fairs are probably being used more now instead of collecting dust.

How do we keep our work simple? It sounds hackneyed, but the answer is to not let our means and ends get out of equilibrium. We should only do work that is necessary to achieve the lifestyle we desire, based on a careful and balanced analysis of our goals, needs, and diversions. If we are aware and if we simplify, most of us don't have to work as hard and as much as we do. The Cimarron Kid believes he has struck a blow for male-liberation in this area.

> It's been my observation that a lot of men work their butts off just to make more money so that their wives and kids can buy what they want. I'm talkin' about excessive wants. It's my feelin' that beyond providin' basic support, the man should let his woman and children buy their own goodies. Let them work for what they want. This helps out women's lib too! Too many men suffer ill health or die young because of this stupid inequality. They shouldn't do it!

When we play we should keep it simple, too, according to OZ. Remember the photographer? You know, when we buy those power drills, power boats, fishing gear, volleyball nets and balls, bicycles, golf and tennis equipment, campers, etc., they begin to possess us. They have to be paid for, insured, stored, cleaned, worried over, transported, set up, taken down, ad infinitum. And most of all they have to be used to be justified—to keep the doubt and guilt away. We have to drill holes, pull water skiers, fish, play ball, tennis and golf, ride and camp whether we want to or not and whether we have the time or not. It wears me out just thinking and writing about it. (And, it will probably wear the reader out as well.)

Another liberating thought occurred to me here. Why do wives and children give men work tools for birthdays, for Father's Day, etc.? And why do husbands and children do the same for the women? Has anyone considered that maybe they really don't want to do the work associated with the tools? Oh well, I digress again. But, if this is stimulating my thinking, then maybe the reader is getting a similar workout. I hope so.

Could it possibly be that some of our complexities result from different forms of aggression? Maybe very subtle and moderate but still one person trying to force their values and perceptions of reality on another. Let's move on to the next chapter and pursue this further.

Chapter 3
NONAGGRESSION

The Code of the West
The Cimarron Kid (1967)

A fellow I used to know,
Thought he was a bloody show.
At actin' like a man he was the best.
He would knock a fellow down,
For sayin' howdy with a frown,
Cause he lived by the code of the West, of the West,
He lived by the code of the West.

Oh, this bloody Texas kid,
Let me tell you what he did.
He shot a Yankee right through the head.
Yes, shot his brains all out,
Without a care or doubt.
And all because this innocent Yankee said, because he said,
And this is what the poor old Yankee said.

"Texans seem so dumb,
Settling arguments with a gun.
A friendly settlement seems to be the best.
It seems stupid and so cruel,
To fight a silly duel.
But to be a man you follow the code of the West, of the West,
You must follow the code of the West."

So, this ignorant Texas child,
In a manner rather wild,
Blew this Yankee all to kingdom come.
Though the advice was sound,
It was offered with a frown.
He'd show them furriners Texans weren't so dumb, weren't so dumb.
He'd show them furriners Texans weren't so dumb.

Now, the Texas boy was hung,
For provin' he wasn't dumb,
And his very last words won't be forgot,
"A murderer I may be,
And also dead you see,
But, I'm proved a man, a coward I am not, I am not.
I'm proved a man, a coward I am not."

Yes, they followed this code,
All the men who rode,
Who rode all over the West's bloody ground.
Violence was needed then,
To prove that men were men,
At least until reason came around, came around,
At least until reason came around.

According to anthropologists,
Philosophers and psychologists,
Man differs from other animals by his cranial capacity.
To build and utilize tools,
Not destroy and act like fools,
Is the way to prove your masculinity, ...inity,
Is the way to prove your masculinity.

So, if you want to be a man,
Then listen while you can.
It's not necessary to fight to prove this fact.
Don't push and don't shove,
Show tolerance and love,
Exhibit knowledge, diplomacy and tact, and tact,
Exhibit knowledge, diplomacy and tact.

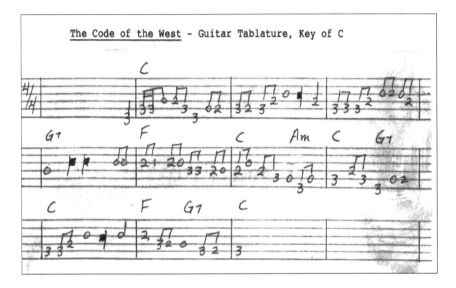

Do you remember from reading the preface that the Cimarron Kid said he used to be a cowboy but he really wasn't? He told me he idolized cowboys when he was young and aspired to being one himself by dressing that way and adopting their mannerisms, their way of talking and their music. He even competed in a rodeo once on a dare. He shied away from the role, however, when it came to riding a horse because he always felt sorry for the horse. He rode from time to time for work and play but he never really liked it.

Do ya really think they enjoy havin' this thing on their back with straps and blankets and such and this other thing jammed in their mouth. Then somebody up there kickin' em in the side and jerkin' their head this-a-way and that? Well, I was never comfortable doin' it for sport or fun. Now, if ya had to do it for survival or to make your livin', that's different.

By the Kid's way of thinking, using anything for our pleasure that requires pain or discomfort to something or somebody is aggression and needs to be reduced or eliminated from our lifestyle if we are to achieve our maximum potential. The cowboy had to live the way he did for the most part but modern-day imitators would do well to resist copying the aggressive aspects of this way of life.

There are, of course, positive, gentle characteristics of this lifestyle. Sadly, the fact that most of the cowboys were honest, hard-working, dependable, brave and quiet individuals who cared a lot for each other and many times went out of their way to be of service to others, is overlooked by many of today's men and women of the West. It often seems that only the attributes of boozing, brawling and hard-riding, oppressive sex are glorified by the media, films and song and are emulated by youthful "pretenders to the throne."

The Cimarron Kid says that the violence in the cowboy image always bothered him and especially does today. But, the romanticism inherent in the Western legends and traditions seldom fails to charm him (or the rest of us, for that matter). The Kid has known many cowboys who were magnificent examples of the best in men about whom he says, "These young pups of today ain't fit to wipe the cowshit off their boots." A prestigious and successful rodeo clown who was a friend of the Kid's in the Fifties, told him this story which illustrates the romantic appeal of the cowboy as well as the aggressive, rowdy lifestyle:

It seems that the cowboy was driving along a deserted stretch of highway in his ramshackle pickup truck. Somewhere between rodeos, he was tooling along, whistling the tune to some old western ballad. He noticed a small boy walking beside the road wearing a huge Stetson hat. The cowboy gave him a lift to the next town complimenting him on his choice of headgear.

The boy smiled as the cowboy asked, "Ya been gettin' in lots of fights lately?"

"No sir!" the boy replied.

"Well, ya been chasin' any of them little girls around?"

"Nope, I haven't," said the boy.

"How about drinkin'? Ya been drinkin' a lot of beer?"

"No sir! I ain't no cowboy, I just found this hat."

The Kid has had an interesting and uncommon evolution concerning aggression and violence. After being an avid hunter and "gun nut" for twenty years, he decided that it was wrong for him to derive pleasure from a sport that hurt other living things. He quit hunting and sold all his guns because of his evolving nonaggression and also because (as mentioned before) of the need to simplify his life. He continued to fish by rationalizing that the intent was to catch the fish, not to kill it. But, he soon realized that this really didn't hold water, so he quit that also. His aggressive behavior has been modified in many ways in the last fifteen years and this is definitely reflected in OZ. If your goal is to increase love and knowledge, then it is hard to justify aggression. His views on this subject are summed up in his universal, all-purpose, nondenominational prayer: "Everything in the Universe is sacred and deserves our tender, loving care."

OZ requires that we apply nonaggression to everything. Nonaggression in this case means to reduce our competition and expression of negative emotions whether they are directed at us, at other people and other living things or at earth, air, fire or water. This involves everything from the Golden Rule to environmentalism. If we love our oceans, lakes and streams, then we won't pollute or waste them by competing with each other and with nature. We will instead work for cooperation with all nature. This stems from the Eastern concept of oneness of all things.

Why does OZ require nonaggression as one of its six methods? Simplicity and awareness seem to have self-evident rationalization for their inclusion in this system. Nonaggression, possibly because it is so alien to our culture, needs more justification and explanation. Usually, nonaggression is part of a moral code where someone or something outside of us demands obedience—"Thou shall not kill." The Kid quotes Gurdjieff on morality, "Morality is like a stick, you can point it this way and that." Morality is relative to the authoritarian system under which a person might operate. OZ prefers to offer practical reasons for practicing nonaggression.

As indicated above, it is a common idea in the East to say that we are all part of the same whole. Pierre Tielhard de Chardin, the free-thinking Jesuit priest, spoke of the Noosphere. He envisioned this to be the sphere of rational thought surrounding the earth, a web of interconnected minds and psyches. The psychiatrist, Carl Jung termed this the Collective Consciousness. The Cimarron Kid calls all this the "Big Brain" and he includes within the Big Brain all of the matter in the Universe. He goes on to say, "If we're all part of each other and of each thing, then that seems to me to be a damn good reason for nonaggression."

The Kid especially asked me to include this little poem he wrote so as to give a scientific view of this idea. That everything, even fundamental particles, is interconnected, interchangeable and recurring:

Twinkle, twinkle little star.
How I wonder what you are.

Hydrogen gas and helium too.
Oh! Now I see—I once was you.
(Astrophysicists have determined that stars are the birthplace of all the atoms in the Universe.)

Nonviolence is a stronger expression of this ideal and has many of its roots in the East. This is a good place to remind the reader that OZ is a blend of East and West. This is apparent here because the practical side of the Kid's philosophy dictates that sometimes violence is necessary; as in all aspects of self-preservation. The Kid says, "I don't wanta kill anything for sport any more but if I'm hungry or if somethin' is tryin' to harm me or mine, I'll drag it to the ground with my teeth if I have to." Therefore, Eastern mysticism is diluted with Western pragmatism.

It might be helpful here to list some of the things that OZ identifies as negative emotions and their method of expression and to explain the large role that competition plays in the game of aggression. We mean to include as negative emotions such things as conceit, greed, worry, distrust, envy, hate, and excessive ambition. Some accompanying expressions of negative emotions are theft, manipulation, physical and mental cruelty, gossip, dishonesty, cheating, waste, inattention and back-biting. These are contrary to OZ whether directed inward or outward and whether at animate or inanimate objects.

Competition is inextricably entangled with aggression. In fact, the Cimarron Kid feels that they are synonymous. We are always competing; with ourselves, with each other and with our environment. Some consider this to be inevitable, natural and desirable for individual and collective well-being. The Kid refuses to accept this and maintains that his own experience has taught him that cooperation instead rarely fails to produce inner and outer benefits for him and for others he has observed. He says, "Course, it depends on your goals. If your goal is wealth, power, fame or control over others, then I guess ya got to compete. But, watch out for the bills; they have a way a comin' due. He who dances must pay the piper. The Gods make people crazy with power when they want to wipe 'em out. The Gods work slowly but they do a damn fine job."

As mentioned in Chapter 1, we do aggress against ourselves. Our health is definitely dependent on our attitude, diet and lifestyle and we are constantly abusing ourselves in these areas. OZ does not tolerate this and we should learn to treat ourselves better. Be more aware of, simplify and slow down or abolish the negative emotions and competition within us.

In the poem which begins the introduction to this book, mention is made of the "Ten O'clock News" as being something wrong with the West. What the Kid meant by this is how we Americans allow an incessant, multi-media barrage of news stories to impinge upon our consciousness daily and in some cases hourly. The distorted view of reality that many of us acquire from all this results in varying degrees of paranoia. I mention this here as a good example of our health suffering from inward expression of negative emotions.

The news in itself is, of course, not evil. But, our unawareness of the various interpretations we and others put on the news as well as the exaggeration and the snowball effect of sensational news stories can cause us to worry needlessly. We fret and stew about the crime rate, the economy, the weather, etc. and we "keep the ball rolling" by discussing all this with our neighbors and friends, usually embellishing and augmenting with little restraint. Awareness and simplicity' can team up here with nonaggression to help us sort things out and not make a "mountain out of a mole hill. Maybe then, the Ten O'clock News won't be so aggressive.

The reader will notice, at this point if not before, that as we move further into this book the boundaries are more ill-defined. They blur and weaken and that is as it should be for OZ is supposed to be a mixture and is supposed to reflect Eastern as well as Western teachings and concepts. Again, we are brought face to face with the idea of unity of the cosmos and we see that awareness, simplicity and nonaggression are all parts of a whole and begin to be more alike and interchangeable the closer they are studied. If we analyze and dissect too much they won't stand still for it and it makes it very difficult to define and systematize. Thus, the Z of OZ; the Zen of Oklahoma Zen. As we continue, it is my hope that I can minimize this intrusion of reality into our fantasy even though I suspect that we will have to tolerate much repetition and overlap.

Aggression is very obvious in most relationships, even loving relationships. Just because this is common and maybe even natural, it does not necessarily follow that we can't or shouldn't work to improve the situation. We should watch ourselves unceasingly to identify our petty emotions and competitions and then try to modify our quarrelsome and troublesome selves so that when we do express anger and fight for our rights and our identity it is in a positive direction. We should trust and love each other more. We should put people over things in our priority list but things should be treated well also.

An example seems necessary here to determine the scope of aggression in our relationships. Sexual aggression is something that affects most of us maddeningly and constantly through most of our lives. A lot of our adverse sexual behavior stems from competition and one-ups-man-ship rather than from our libido. This was alluded to in the previous chapter as misuse of sexual energy. A current trend in America is to rate, grade and improve everyone's sexual performance. The essence of love is cooperation and not competition. After all, we **are** "making love." What difference does it make how we stack up in the Indy 500 (or should we say the Las Vegas 10) of sex. The important thing is to please ourselves and each other and to grow closer in the process (see next chapter—Growth), not to find acceptance in the world of *Playboy* or *Cosmopolitan* magazines.

OZ considers sexual competition as a form of aggression that runs the gamut from innocuous things like flirtation and posturing to disastrous and hurtful situations such as manipulation, cheating and even rape. It would be idiocy to try to keep ourselves from flirting and from flaunting ourselves, this does little comparable harm anyway, but there are many reasons why we could and should attempt to diminish our use of sex as a means of ego-gratification through competition. The

Cimarron Kid feels that many people who have love affairs outside of marriage do so not because of their sex drive but because they are starved for adventure and want to show off their various abilities ("If it ain't natural, it's unnatural").

An extreme example of the omnipresence of sex and how it contributes to so much because of its force and its universality was noted by Gurdjieff who said,

> "At the same time sex plays a tremendous role in maintaining the mechanicalness of life. Everything that people do is connected with 'sex': politics, religion, art, the theater, music, is all 'sex'! Do you think people go to the theater or to church to pray or to see some new play? That is only for the sake of appearances. The principal thing, in the theater as well as in church, is that there will be a lot of women or a lot of men. This is the center of gravity of all gatherings. What do you think brings people to cafes, to restaurants, to various fetes? One thing only. SEX: it is the principal force of all mechanicalness. All sleep, all hypnosis, depends on it."

Sleep and hypnosis in this context can be equated to unawareness in the OZ system. The Kid believes that this unawareness coupled with the tremendous force and universality of sex causes us a lot of misery and discomfort. Through the practice of OZ we might alleviate some of this.

Do we compete with our homes and clothing? Certainly! And, we use them to aggress against our fellow humans and nature. In America, we use far more resources than is necessary for comfort and beauty in producing our houses and attire ("too many shoes"). We also compete with each other and ourselves in trying for bigger, better, prettier, different and more expensive. Our over-use of resources and our refusal to recycle materials on a meaningful scale is harmful to nature and our fellow humans. International relations suffer when it becomes apparent that with something like only five percent of the world's population, we use a hugely disproportionate share of its resources. This is a form of aggression. Waste, endemic to the West, is an even more blatant example of making war on each other and our environment.

There are countless opportunities to find competition and expression of negative emotions in our work and our play. Most of these will be obvious to the thinking reader when he or she ponders the many games, careers, recreation and entertainment with which we are all involved. I am going to concentrate at this point on the aggression that is rampant in our money-making and money-spending, materialistic society. I'm referring to what a character in Tom Robbins' book. *Another Roadside Attraction*, calls "Economic Totalitarianism." Don't get uptight, dear reader, this is not an indictment of capitalism! The practice of Economic Totalitarianism (hereinafter referred to as ET) knows no political or ideological bounds. The Soviets suffer as much from this as we do.

Most of us: leaders or followers, socialists or capitalists, city dwellers or rural types, rich or poor, educated or illiterate, North or South or East or West, practice ET which is a method of decision-making whereby money is always given first priority. Budgetary concerns take precedence every time over such "mundane" things as health and the well-being of people and of the rest of the Universe. OZ seeks to alter this slightly for those persons who see that ET represents a monstrous imbalance that can and does cause irreparable harm to all it touches. According to the Kid, this may be the most insidious and destructive form of aggression that we experience. He's trying to slow down the momentum of this negative force in his own life but he says, "It's like tryin' to give a wild cow an enema. Even if ya succeed ya still have a hell-uva mess to clean up. I reckon it's worth it though. The real hard part is convincin' others of the worth of it so they'll at least leave you alone in tryin' to clean up your act or, better yet, they might give it a try too."

Rather than use "bigger than life" situations such as proliferation of nuclear weapons, over-population, pollution, famine, etc., let's examine how ET monopolizes the life of the common man like you and me.

Imagine this lady who has worked at her job for thirty years and is eligible for early retirement. She is suffering from several job-stress-related ailments but decides to keep working because she needs the extra monetary benefits that a few more years will buy. You know the rest of the story! She dies before her retirement and all for a measly few dollars ("Too many bucks"). She made her decision in favor of wealth over health and the only people who will profit economically are possibly her heirs.

A less tragic story, but with the same lesson, would be a man who is offered much better pay if he will move himself and his family to another city, the location of a branch of the firm for which he is working. Let's sweeten the deal and let him move up to management level as well. No one in his family wants to make the move. The children don't want to leave their school and friends. He and his wife are apprehensive about leaving for a number of reasons, not the least of which is the family's very active interest in mountain sports and they are leaving Colorado for Louisiana. They also can't tolerate heat and humidity. But, our hero, like most of us, opts for the money. ET has struck again.

A final example might be a city manager for a small Midwestern town faced with a decision to recommend to the city council the fate of a certain parcel of land under his jurisdiction. He has to decide whether to suggest that the land be used for a park which is badly needed by the people of the town or be designated as a site for a factory that some corporation wants to locate in his area. He decides in favor of the factory even though he and his own family are well aware of the urgent requirement for parkland in the town. The added tax money for the town's coffers and the promise of additional employment tip the scales.

OZ does not insist that all decisions be made without considering money. It just asks that we work for balance, which is obviously lacking in most cases today, and to try to achieve some small victories over the aggression that we do in the name of money. We should be **aware** of these problems and how much competition and expression of negative emotions are causal factors here. We should **simplify** the situation so that understanding and action is more easily accomplished. And, we should make sure that we **reduce the aggression** in and around us.

Chapter 4
GROWTH

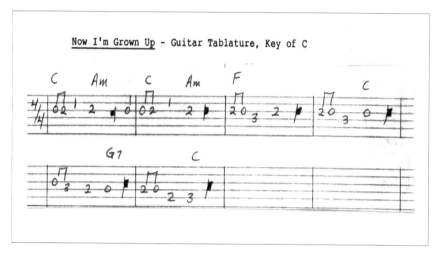

Now I'm Grown Up - Guitar Tablature, Key of C

Here's a couple of songs that the Cimarron Kid wrote in 1967 about some of his personal growth:

Now I'm Grown
The Cimarron Kid

When I was young,
I used to have fun.
Now I am old,
I carry a load,
Worry too much,
Carry a crutch.
[Spoken] You know, there's somethin' screwy here.
To become an adult ya got to grow up—learn to be
responsible. How many responsible adults have you
seen lately? Intolerance, hypocrisy, status-seekers,
indifference, apathy, dishonesty, greed, pollution, waste,

litter, ... MAN! Talk about irresponsibility and misguided children; don't do as I do, do as I say.

Used to travel around,
From town to town.
Didn't cost me a dime,
I had a good time.
But, now I'm grown up,
My life's in a rut.
[Spoken] What did it cost me anyway to hitch a ride,
bathe in the river, sleep on the ground?
I used to be real.
I used to could feel.
Didn't think of money.
Now, ain't that funny?
Didn't worry about status,
Or people who hate us.
[Spoken] I was kinda different then; now I have
to work at it.

I been such a phony,
Been ridin' the wrong pony.
It's time to change horses,
To join the youthful forces.
Of status I'll be rid.
I'll live like a kid.
[Spoken] Who says ya can't do it in midstream anyway?

Through all of our years,
We just don't have ears,
Content in our roles,

Sellin' our souls,
Keepin' up with the Jones,
Keepin' up with their loans,
[Spoken] Kids are just childlike; adults are childish!

I died somewhere,
Somewhere back there.
Forgot how to feel.
Lost my ideal.
My spirit I did lose.
That's what causes the blues.
[Spoken] But .... I shall be born again!

No longer a pup,
I'm truly grown up.
No longer in the gutter.
No longer in a clutter.
I'm no longer a sham,
"I yam what I yam."
[Spoken] That's what Popeye always said—that old
cartoon-strip existentialist. I'm free! The best things
in life are free. I don't know who said that but let
me tell ya what I say, "In a spiritual sense, the best
things in life cost like hell." But, it's all worth it. Try it,
you'll like it.

(See music for "Now I'm Grown Up" on page 75)

The Search, an Okie's Tribute to Zen
Tune: Pretty Polly

I've walked all around boys,
And what did I find.
I've walked all around boys,
And what did I find.
Great God a'mighty,
I couldn't ease my mind.

I've searched through your mountains,
I've searched through your sea.
I've searched through your mountains,
I've searched through your sea.
And, all I ever found.
Was people just like me.

I've searched through your churches,
And temples so fair.
I've searched through your churches,
And temples so fair.
I asked all your preachers,
But nothing was there.

I've worked in the country,
I've worked on your farm.
I've worked in the country,
I've worked on your farm.
And all I ever found,
Was the muscle in my arm.

I've roamed and I've rambled,
And hunted your land.
I've roamed and I've rambled,
And hunted your land.
And all I ever found,
Was a self-centered man.

Then, I saw a little man,
Sittin' down by the road.
I saw a little man,
Sittin' down by the road.
I asked him where to go.
To unburden my load.

[Spoken] And, this is what he said to me:

Education, and travel,
And learnin' is fine.
Education, and travel.
And learnin' is fine.
But, ya got to look inside, boy,
To find peace of mind.

I looked deep inside,
For this secret so rare.
I looked deep inside,
For this secret so rare.
Magnificent Buddha,
The answer was there.

I looked into my soul, boys,
And what did I find.
I looked into my soul, boys,
And what did I find.
Holy Minerva,
I found peace of mind.

To grow, to live,
To follow the plan.
To grow, to live,
To follow the plan.
You must look inside, boys.
To really see the man.

In the OZ system, escape is the inverse of growth. If we employ the jargon of the East we would say escape is the Yin or dark force and growth is the Yang or light force. We will define escape in this book as any activity that requires little or no physical or mental attention or any activity with which we are involved so frequently and for such duration that they divert our attention from other important functions and endeavors. Balance is very important here. In fact, any imbalance in our life might be a clue that we are indulging too much or, and this is important, too little in escape activities.

Many things we do could fall within the above definition: entertainment, recreation, hobbies, work, sex, shopping, talking, daydreaming, sleeping and drugs to name a few. Of course, all of these can also be growth experiences. The difference usually is determined by the quality and quantity of the activity.

The balance for which we should be alert and for which we should strive is our own growth/escape ratio. We must determine our own needs in this area and be sure we don't confuse ambition with growth. We must also recognize that growth in itself can be an escape. Even though, when used properly it is the enemy of sleep, it can also become mechanical and lure us away from the harmony necessary for OZ. Work-a-holics, through their frantic devotion to their work, to the extent of forgetting and foregoing all else, are a good illustration of this phenomenon.

The Kid always says, concerning growth.

It just means to keep on truckin', but use an old truck. Make sure that your truck requires a lot of attention. It can't be one of them new-fangled jobs that can go anywhere, anytime and almost looks after itself. Your truck should work real good but ya ought to have to stop ever so often to check the oil and everything. If ya don't, it just keeps on truckin' while ya sleep!

In other words, growth is evolution and perseverance in all facets of our lives but not to the point that it becomes either compulsive, frantic or mechanical.

We must constantly be aware of growth and keep it simple and goal-oriented. We should also be sure that through our growth efforts we aren't involved in aggressive behavior towards ourselves or others. And, to achieve maximum OZ growth, we actively and consciously seek our own level by having enough escape in all parts of our lives to help us reach our goals and to insure an adequate amount of joy in the process.

The idea of growth comes more from the Cimarron Kid's Western background and upbringing than it does from his studies of the East. He felt that to make OZ a complete and harmonious system and in order for it to have practical and progressive aspects, that growth should be included. Not that there is not growth in the East; we aren't speaking of the East of Toyota, Sony, Yamaha, Mitsubishi, etc. which are relatively new phenomena and are basically patterned on Western concepts of research, production and marketing. We're referring here to traditional, oriental customs and attitudes of "sitting and watching the crazy Western world rush by" and contemplating navels. These approaches to life, fostered by Buddhism, Hinduism, Yoga and Tai Chi Chuan, these meditative and essentially passive paths are a very important ingredient in OZ. But, in the Kid's opinion are too static and selfish when taken alone. They cause us to be mired down in self and don't allow enough interconnection with "Big Brain." They don't promote, by themselves, the Kid's goals of expansion of love and knowledge. But, without Eastern awareness, simplicity and nonviolence, then the atmosphere is not correct for realizing goals either. Therefore, with growth and with the addition of service and joy, we move closer to a complete and balanced system.

We can use the Cimarron Kid as an example of OZ growth concerning physical health. Over the years, he has developed a regimen that insures total fitness, that is balanced, aware, simple, nonaggressive, joyful and that allows for growth, service and escape. The Kid has combined Yoga, Tai Chi, jogging, hiking, walking, swimming and calisthenics into a loosely organized program. It exercises his cardiovascular system by increasing his pulse rate to a prescribed level and maintaining that level for twenty to twenty-five minutes, three times a week. It stretches, flexes and strengthens all his body. It works on his balance and endurance. It also includes meditation and awareness exercises. And, it's fun, so the Kid tells me. (All these exercises will be detailed in the Appendix along with other suggestions for incorporating OZ into your life.)

As hinted above, the Kid's fitness growth includes aspects that work on mental and emotional growth:

> I meditate when I'm doin' my Yoga and Tai Chi, which is kind of an escape. It relaxes me. But, I also use them to make myself aware of all of me and to talk myself outa bein' sick. I concentrate on my blood, my nerves, my vision, my hearing, taste and smell and on whatever's buggin' me physically or mentally. It helps me solve my problems. I also chant sometimes (AUM MANE PADME HUM) when I'm doin' my Yoga or even runnin' or swimmin'. It helps center me with the rhythms and vibrations of

nature. The primitive folks knew, and know, about vibrations and Gurdjieff talked about 'em too. Ya know what I mean—stompin' and dancin' and drum-beatin' and singin' and chantin' and the blood flowin' and the seasons and birth and death and rain and clouds and wind and ...

The three precepts of Tai Chi Chuan—circle, continuity and equilibrium—seem to fit in here with what the Kid is jabbering about.

What about physical growth imbalance? We return to the poor, old jogger for an illustration. Often, when people get involved with something like jogging they become addicted to it. This can be a positive addiction if it doesn't disrupt the harmony necessary for total self in OZ. The jogger, especially those folks who began running later in life, gets such satisfying and immediate benefits in fitness and appearance that he or she pushes for greater challenges and supposedly greater benefits. They run faster and farther and often begin competing (there we go again) and trying more difficult terrain. Ego takes over and many times people lose sight of their original fitness goals. Many things can get "out of kilter" and even permanent injury can result. I've spoken to spouses who say that their mate's sex drive has lessened or disappeared. The reason we're picking on the jogger so much is because the Kid went through much of this pattern himself before he wised up and backed off to a more reasonable level. "My truck was too mechanical and too well-oiled. I just kept on a'rollin', faster and faster, until the truck was drivin' me. Now, I'm master! Hope so, anyway."

Another situation where the ego got in the way of physical growth was the Cimarron Kid's experiences with downhill skiing. In 1968, I asked him why he didn't ski. "Because everybody else does," he replied. I said, "Why, that's nothing but reverse snobbery." He answered, "I believe you're right, Hudi." The very next day he went skiing. In the interim he has found that he really doesn't care that much for downhill skiing but the reasons now are experientially-based and not because of his weird elitism. "I like cross-country skiing all right, but I'd still rather be swimmin' in an old farm pond as to be out in all that cold and have to mess with all the paraphernalia and stuff."

Intellectually, we must grow and evolve in order to keep the "wheels of the truck rollin'." We can do this in a number of ways, through education in its multiple forms, through work and play, reading, hobbies, relationships, thinking, observing, playing games, solving puzzles, etc. But, OZ insists that we not be lazy here. We must be aware and then act.

What happens when we are lazy with our intellectual growth? The problems that may result are myriad. Our mental and physical health can deteriorate. Senility, stagnation and boredom are common. Relationships may suffer. Our work and play might begin to drag and aggression against ourselves and others may become evident. Accidents may increase.

But, remember balance! If we get too involved in intellectual pursuits, the same problems can result. We have to factor into our personal equation enough escape activities to achieve the proper blend. Some people who refuse to watch television are typical examples of imbalance toward intellectual growth. Although there is plenty of trash on television, even that can be helpful when you need to take your mind out of gear and just kick back and vegetate awhile. Football games seem to be very good for this and the fact that some pointy-headed intellectuals tend to poke fun at the television football fan attests to the therapeutic value of the pastime.

Growth in emotional health takes place in the OZ system by learning to express negative emotions less and less as we grow older and hopefully wiser. This is no less important than growth in other areas, but from discussion of non-expression of negative emotions in preceding chapters, it is hoped that the reader already has an understanding of this concept. Turn to the Appendix if you want to see how this works on a practical, day-to-day level.

Growth in relationships pays very large dividends. This growth is most valuable when we grow in understanding and empathy. To know someone, in whatever context; in the biblical sense, culturally, artistically, professionally, child to parent, parent to child, as brother or sister, as a friend, as an enemy, as a teacher, as a student, as husband or wife, and to know them wholly, totally and completely, is a veritable treasure. To develop an affinity with someone to the point approaching, and in some respects reaching, extra-sensory perception is a peak experience of the first order. In this sense, love and knowledge become one, which is all part of the plan.

If we extend this growing and knowing, this love and knowledge, to everything in the Universe ("Everything is sacred and deserves our tender, loving care") then we approach the pinnacle of OZ, at least according to the Kid's goals. This is similar to what Pierre Tielhard called the "Omega Point," which the Kid explains as the time when the consciousness of all matter in the cosmos is raised to the level at which everything is aware of itself and everything else. This is comparable to Nirvana; Heaven, the Age of Aquarius and so on. But wait, we stray into the metaphysical and that is not our intent. Back to basics.

We should grow in work and play. This seems to go without saying. If for no other reason, growth should occur here just to avoid boredom. But, growth at the office or factory and on the playing grounds or in our recreation rooms will help us do more than stay interested in our pursuits. Here's where competition gets some good press. Balance! Balance! Balance!

We all need challenges and variety. The Kid says one of the most important things a teacher can recognize is the need for variety in pupils of all ages. We should, even in OZ, compete with ourselves to the extent that we try new things, improve the old, and try something crazy and off-the-wall once in awhile. We must keep ourselves vital until the day we die. Otherwise, we're already dead. You've heard this before. It is necessary, though, to recognize its importance in OZ.

At work we should try new problem-solving and design techniques. We could request new work schedules, work partners or locations. We might change jobs or careers. Familiarity breeds contempt. We might grow by simply changing the way we talk and listen when we interact with colleagues, superiors or someone we supervise. We could dress differently or change our office decor or routine.

At play, we should learn new skills, crafts and hobbies. New games and sports help us grow. Force yourself into uncomfortable situations concerning entertainment and recreation and see how you react. Sometimes the worst of situations teach us the most and are responsible for considerable growth. Gurdjieff called this "conscious suffering." The Cimarron Kid says it has been very painful but enlightening to him to include this in his growth plan. Accidental suffering is anathema to OZ but to purposefully set up discomforting and irritable situations that have growth potential is a "horse of a different color."

But, wait again. You're probably already familiar with these lists of suggestions for rekindling or continuing the zest for life. Just keep in mind that you mustn't go overboard. Keep it simple and balanced. Challenge and variety should be our servants, not our masters.

Chapter 5
SERVICE

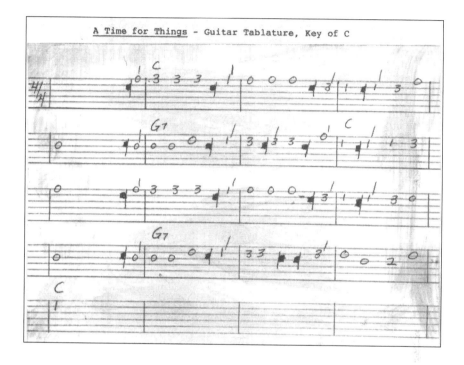

A Time for Things - Guitar Tablature, Key of C

A Time for Things
The Cimarron Kid (1968)

The stream is twistin', rollin' down,
Onto the gentle plain.
The wild bird cries and hearkens to,
The misty mornin' rain.
The beer cans all are rusting,
Where they have shortly lain.
The time has come for beauty,
And we've spoiled it once again.

The little stream is given birth,
Away up in the hills.
Where baby trout, are born again,
And play among her rills.
The poisoned water we have made,
Flows darkly through their gills.
The time has come for living,
But, I fear it only kills.

A man is coming home from work,
His aim is to unwind.
His little children want to play,
Their happiness to find.
His wife she wants to talk to him,
To ease her troubled mind.
The time has come for love,
But, he just can't find the time.

Now, there are questions asked of men,
Appealing to the wise.
Why do we have war,
And pollution in our skies?
Where do babies come from,
Asks a child with innocent eyes?
The time has come for truth,
But, the answers all are lies.

Now, I've seen many a sunset,
As I've traveled through each year.
But, man's atomic sunset,
It fills me so with fear.

There is a warning to all men,
But, some men just won't hear.
The time has come for crying,
But, I just can't find a tear.

Now, man must learn and man must know,
So what will be his fate?
Will he heed the warning,
Before it is too late?
Will he understand his brother,
Will he no longer hate?
The time has come for hope,
And I hope that we'll have faith.

"I'll pass it on down the line." This is what a decrepit, old bum told the Kid after he had given the hitchhiker a ride one cold, blustery day out of Stillwater, Oklahoma. It seems the Kid was driving north to see his girlfriend when he spied the old man shuffling along the road with his thumb limply thrust into the air out over the shoulder of the highway. He stopped to pick him up, noticing his ragged, ill-fed condition. Taking the offered cigarette, the bum mentioned that he hadn't had a smoke, or for that matter, anything to eat for quite a spell. Twelve miles down the road they pulled into "Bill's Corner," a small eatery and a gas station set up on a crossroads. The Kid bought the hitchhiker a hamburger, coffee and pie and watched with concern and curiosity as with shaking hands the bum fed himself. As he dropped the man off twelve more miles down the road, the Kid heard something he would remember the rest of his life. The hitchhiker accepted the rest of the pack of cigarettes and said, "Thanks Bo, I'll pass it on down the line."

Passing it on down the line is the essence of service in the OZ system. This is yet another variation on the theme of the Golden Rule. The Cimarron Kid was amazed at the simplicity and beauty of this "code of the road"; you make sure that good deeds are kept cycling through all your buddies and chance acquaintances and thus eventually through all of humanity. The anti-entropic powers of love and caring are amplified and spread everywhere, much the same way bad news and evil deeds are communicated. Of course, this idea had been pounded into the Kid at Sunday school, church and home, but to see it in action was something else.

In Oklahoma Zen, this idea of service applies not only to our fellow humans but to everything else. It embodies the environmental ethic and requires us to not only have care for everything but to also act on that concern. No lip-service here! To be of service to each other and to the Cosmos, we should be aware, keep things simple, reduce aggression, provide for growth and actively perform good deeds in all aspects of our daily living. All done with joy!

If we look for opportunities to be a good neighbor, no matter how small and insignificant they may appear to be, then a more livable, lovable world is possible.

The readers will say at this point, "Hey! I've heard that somewhere before." And they will be right. Very little in this book is original if taken by itself. The composite, balanced whole is, however, original, we think, and worthwhile. Service, though considered corny and old-fashioned by some, is a significant part of OZ. And, unlike the emphasis on assertiveness and the "me first" approach that abounds today, OZ maintains that we must let down our defenses, increase our trust and risk-taking and purposefully return to these old teachings. We are in this together and through cooperation we will continue to grow toward long-anticipated ideals of peace and brotherhood.

The Kid says he feels compelled to be of service to others because of Big Brain. It makes so much sense to him to "keep it churnin' and grindin' in the mill." By adding our small part to the total cooperation of Big Brain, we increase the capacity for love and knowledge and help insure steady evolution in these areas. Oddly enough, even though service is traditionally thought of as a non-selfish act, in this sense we are thinking of ourselves. We are helping ourselves by helping others and the motivation is not altruism, not morality based on divine guidance, but simply self-preservation and self-progression. We grow through group as well as individual action.

The idea of service in OZ is definitely more Western oriented than Eastern. Many of the Eastern teachings stress individualism and detachment to the point of subverting John Donne's famous statement, "No man is an island." They seem to flaunt the idea that we are not dependent on each other as we follow our own paths to wherever we're going. This seems to be in direct contrast to the idea of the unity of all things and has always puzzled the Kid. He says:

> I think we can learn a lot from our good buddies in the East with all their ideas about not gettin' too involved, not lettin' the blood get up with care and worry over others and things. But, some folks use this as a cop-out. They seem to need an excuse for not helpin' out so they just say, "Oh Man! I can't get involved with savin' the whales or stoppin' the arms race. I'm into Zen, or each man must find his own path, or that's too material or establishment or whatever." It's sometimes a haven for laziness or self-worship.

This is not to imply that Easterners are not good neighbors or that they don't serve each other. On the contrary, many examples of gentleness, politeness and acts of great sacrifice can be found throughout the world regardless of culture or nationality. What we are saying here is that some Eastern teachings that have found a certain degree of popularity here in the West in the last twenty or thirty years do not stress service as an important part of their discipline. Western teachings generally do even though they often tend to go overboard.

This is a good place to remind the reader about equilibrium. In being of service we have to maintain that fine balance that is so crucial to OZ. If we get drawn into the "do-gooder" syndrome, then we use too much energy here and lose the harmony necessary to seek our goals.

We have to learn to say no and to shepherd our resources so they are used evenly and effectively. This is one of the faults that often is evident with people active in service clubs and church and charity groups. They get so involved in helping others they often forget to help themselves and their families and friends. Then, they're no good to anyone, sometimes even becoming a negative force.

Our health blossoms when we are of service to anything, organic or inorganic, spiritual or material. This is catching! Other people follow your example or are just cheered by your actions. A big factor in the OZ concept of service is to be an example. If we act rather than talk and if our actions bring positive results, then others will follow suit. Physical fitness provides a good example here. The more joggers there are, the more joggers there are. We must be careful here, though. The "herd instinct" is not proper motivation for OZ. Remember, inner direction is very important. Still, serving as an example can break the ice and expose people to activities and ideas of which they might otherwise be ignorant or choose to ignore.

For our own health and for the health of others we should serve as examples of right eating, right exercise, right thinking and right expression of emotions. All of this in balance with other services and with the other methods of OZ.

We can probably give more service through our relationships than in any other way. Sharing and giving have always been part of the American way. OZ asks that we expand on this. The Cimarron Kid says one of the reasons for this book is to share what he thinks is important with his family and friends. He also told me to include this anecdote about his friend Scotty (the hitchhiking buddy in the song, "Travelin' Blues" included in the introduction to this book) that illustrates a way of sharing few of us would even think about, let alone act on.

In 1965, the Kid and Scotty were hiking into an old mining area on the Kootenai River up by Eureka, Montana. Scotty was interested in the possibilities of some gold prospecting in the area and had asked the Kid to use his knowledge of geology to help him out. They came upon this mine site that looked as if it had been totally untouched ever since its abandonment, probably in the 1920s or 1930s.

Usually, as we all know, these places have been thoroughly explored and picked over and it was with some excitement that these two romantics carefully examined their find. One item of particular interest was a handmade wheelbarrow, including a wooden wheel that still retained the ax marks left in the shaping. Since it was largely intact and preserved, the Kid wanted to pack it out for use as a planter. His wife would love it.

As he started to pick up the object of interest, Scotty exclaimed, "Let's just leave it as it is. Kid."

The Kid replied, "You crazy injun. (Scotty is part Choctaw/Chickasaw.) Ya think we're goin' to disturb the ancient spirits of this place or somethin'?"

"Nothin' religious about it, Kid, it's just gotta be left alone."

"Why?"

"I can't explain it, but we might have to wrestle over it if ya try to take it!"

Now, the Kid had already had a tussle with Scotty (in the eighth grade) which he painfully lost, so he carefully reconsidered the situation. After a little thought, for practical as well as philosophical reasons, he relented. Years later he began to see the wisdom in all this and it couldn't be attributed only to Scotty's Indian heritage. It was just Scotty's way of being of service to fellow travelers, to the past and to the future. The Kid says he learned a lot from Scotty and from this one example alone he has developed a policy which has stopped his collecting urges and which has by and large been responsible for his habit of leaving all manner of things totally unbothered. Ironically, this also helped lead the Kid to the conclusion to quit hunting and fishing, in which sports Scotty ardently and actively participates to this day.

As another example of service from, a slightly different perspective, I would like to tell two stories about my brother-in-law, John E. He's one tough Okie, but there are many people indebted to John E. for his various and sometimes "off-the-wall" good deeds. He can be rude and crude at times but he has a big heart and he certainly, without any knowledge of this philosophy, has done more than his share of service in the tradition of OZ. I could never perform most of the services he has, at least not as effectively or effortlessly as he has done them. But, that's all right. OZ says to serve, but each in his own way.

John E. owned a restaurant at one time in his life.

While out among the patrons, telling stories with a characteristic "good-ole-boy" banter, he happened to notice a lady choking on a piece of meat. Now 1 would have been leery about interfering and embarrassed about making a scene, but not John E. Where angels fear to tread, he builds an interstate highway. He literally leaped to the rescue before the lady's astonished husband even began to move. Not bothering with any questions or answers, he thrust his fingers down her throat and pulled out the vagrant piece of meat. Now, that's service! How many of us could duplicate this?

I could tell hundreds of stories about John E., dozens of which involve service to others, but one more will suffice here. Simplicity, remember?

John. E. was watching television in his Jockey briefs one warm spring evening when the door crashed open and in burst his neighbor with whom he was barely acquainted. She ran right up to the couch and screamed, "My baby has eaten Super Glue!" Now, you have to picture John E. He's no small man and his underwear, which would be regular style on me, was a bikini on him. He, again without stopping for niceties, jumped up, ran across his yard in full view and grabbing a dish washing sponge out of the sink, forced it into the baby's mouth. Fortunately, the glue had only gotten on the lips and teeth of the child and hadn't set-up yet. Service, with-a capital S.

We can be of service to our family, friends and strangers in so many ways. We can teach, provide examples, discipline, advise and help with any number and type of chores and hardships. We can listen more and try to understand more. We can attempt to see things as others see them. We can do little things like allowing someone to move in line, or change lanes in traffic or something big such as visiting a nursing home on a regular basis and sharing ourselves with the lonely folks who happen to be there.

We can also work on improving our relationships with animals, plants and inanimate matter by recognizing their needs and the effects of our actions upon them. We can try to coexist with them so that we leave them alone in the tradition of Scotty or at least have minimum negative impact on them.

We can be of service through our living in our homes, yards and clothing by consuming less and recycling more. By conserving energy and resources, we not only directly embrace our world with love and care, we also show others we care and sometimes help them see the way. There are other concrete, specific suggestions for practicing OZ service in this area as well as others in the Appendix.

Through our work we can develop ourselves so that we, through service along with awareness, simplicity, nonaggression, growth and joy, cooperate more and compete less. Some of the disservices that occur in the workplace, such as gossip, manipulation, social and career climbing, back stabbing, etc. are obvious places to begin. Also, we can be of great service to our fellow humans if we conscientiously and effectively work to reduce our ambitions and aspirations. In the best spirit of OZ, we shouldn't be so concerned about making more money, impressing the boss or the opposite sex or achieving career goals at the expense of others or ourselves. Moonlighting, for instance, takes a job away from others who might need it more. This is heady stuff for those who agree and probably maddening for those who don't. In any case we would agree that cutting back on your successes, ambitions and salary is very advanced OZ work. This is only for those who have reached the rank of Master-Yellow Belt status. There are no OZ Masters, as of this writing.

The Kid told me to be sure and add something here about his own dedication to service. He said that change had occurred concerning his musical performances just while he was getting this chapter straight in his head so I could get it recorded correctly in this book. For the past several years his desire to perform his music had been decreasing steadily. This, was partly due to some bad experiences with organizers of concerts and partly because of human relations with other musicians. Also, the ego-compulsion to "show off" his skills had diminished somewhat (although you would hardly notice it) and he had just about decided to quit all the hassle and stress associated with "pickin' and grinnin' for hire or for charity." "Sometimes, the folks who wanted ya to play free treated ya the worst," said the Kid. "I never will understand why. Ya were givin' of yourself as best ya could and they just stomped all over ya!"

The Cimarron Kid was asked to provide campfire music at a Fourth of July celebration near Aspen, Colorado one summer. Even though the people who were hosting the party were friends, he was a bit reluctant to attend. He always enjoyed the music and knew others did too, but for reasons mentioned above and because of what he now calls a "phony humility" he was concerned about the whole affair. He says, "It turned out great. The people were beautiful and we had a real whing-ding of a party."

The incident ultimately responsible for his change of mind about performing in general happened as he and his family were leaving the next day for the return journey to Boulder, Colorado.

The host, Peter, was thanking the Kid for the music and began telling him how he would like to turn this into an annual affair. Peter, who had suffered a bout with polio and a serious accident which had further weakened him, owns a large portion of the Roaring Fork Valley downstream from Aspen. Physically crippled but materially blessed, he might have been a bitter, selfish man. Definitely not! He was speaking to the Kid of his wish to, in the face of rampant development in the Aspen area, maintain his land as it had always been for the sake of history and stability. In addition, he expressed the desire to include the old-timers and locals in the valley in his plans and at his parties. "I want to honor them," he said, "and let them know that someone cares for them, for their land and their ways. You know, they've worked their butts off on this land and they really love it but they sometimes feel left out with all the changes. Your music could really help me achieve these goals Kid, and I want you to plan, if you want to, to be back here next July 4th."

The Kid said that was one of those times when something just sort of snapped and he saw things in a new light:

I felt lower than a lizard crawlin' on the sands of Death Valley. Here I got a part of my philosophy called service and I'm startin' to be a real asshole about sharin' myself. If ya got talents, ya should share 'em and I intend to do that from now on. And, I intend to be quick about it too—faster than a dose of salts through a government mule. Ya see Hudi, this here study of mine, this Oklahoma Zen is just gettin' started. I gotta helluva long way to go. And, ya know, music is so much fun and joyful which is an important part of OZ, and there I was, inconsistent as usual.

As we see above, we can be of service through our playful activities as well. Various talents, hobbies and skills in the arts and other forms of entertainment, in athletics, and in recreation can be given and shared with everything with which we come in contact. Even though we often have to sacrifice time and other resources to accomplish these services, they should always be done in a joyful way—the subject of the next chapter.

Chapter 6
JOY

The Things I Love
The Cimarron Kid (1967)

The things I love,
Are simple things.
And they belong to each and everyone.
They are all hidden,
But can be found.
If you will look they can be won.

An old pine tree,
It preaches of wisdom,
And a wild bird is crying truth.
An old black kettle,
Tells of the past,
And is a grave for coyote's tooth.

A misty rain,
The sound of frogs,
And a walk with a ragged bum.
A good hard run,
That works my lungs,
And the sound of a guitar's strum.

The smile of a child,
A lovers' touch.
The smell of my love's hair.

A talk with friends,
A talk with nature,
A talk with a mountain way up there.

The flight of a bird,
The surge of a fish,
Tied fast to my fly line.
He gets away,
Or he is caught,
Either way I am his and he is mine.

A cup of tea,
Hot and dark,
Boiled in an old tin can.
A crackling fire,
Ringed with stones,
Shining on my true love's hand.

A candle's glow,
A shadow's face,
And the joy of making something new.
The time to think,
The time to love,
These things belong to me and you.

The things I love,
Are simple things,
And they belong to each and every kind.
They are all hidden,
But can be found,
If you will seek, then you will find.

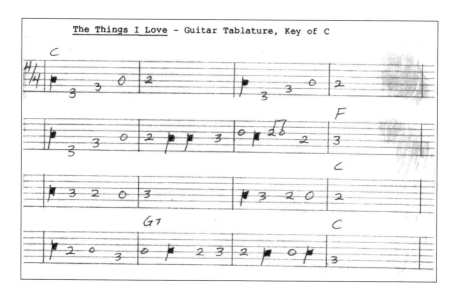

The Things I Love - Guitar Tablature, Key of C

"Come with Me," Said He
Ed McCurdy, Balladeer

"Come with me," said he.
"Come with you," said she,
"Oh, where sir?"

"To my chambers," said he.
"To your chambers," said she,
"Oh, why sir?"

"Cause I'll have ya," said he.
"Cause you'll have me," said she,
"Oh, why sir?"

"Cause I like it," said he.
"Cause you like it," said she,
[Pause] .... "So do I!"

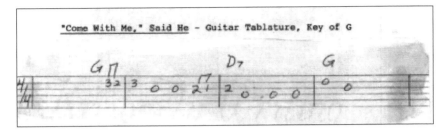

The songs above epitomize the OZ method, Joy. The second song was found written on a monastery wall somewhere in Europe and put to music by McCurdy. At least this is what he told the audience as he was performing in the early 1960s, at a coffee house. The Buddhi, in Oklahoma City. The Cimarron Kid was present that evening and was very amused and impressed with the song regardless of its source. He says, "Here we have a meetin' of minds and bodies; mutual pleasure without game-playin' or guilt. Now, that's fun and good for ya too!" The Kid also remembers McCurdy's introduction to the singing of "Twinkle, Twinkle Little Star." He asked the crowd to sing-a-long with him telling them not to feel self-conscious about singing a children's song. "This isn't being childish," he said, "it's being childlike; there is an immense difference. It's a joy to be childlike at any age."

To be childlike is also part of the focus of this chapter. Most of us are too serious and too busy, especially with philosophical endeavors. It seems that many pleasant things that harm no one are suppressed, ignored, forgotten or considered sinful as we mature and grow older. Going barefoot, playing in the mud, singing, dancing, joking, laughing, crying, touching, hugging, loving. The poet and mystic, William Blake, wrote of men in a future time, looking back in history and being amazed that "... love, sweet love was thought a crime." Witness the grim-faced ascetics of the world, these self-proclaimed saviors of men's souls, of the environment, and of our nationality, our pride, our politics and our economics. These fanatic, true-believers may represent worthwhile causes but they get so caught up in them that the Kid refers to them as "tight-asses who don't want to have fun and don't want anyone else to either." The Kid adds:

> I know of what I speak. I have an awful ten-
> dency to be a true-believer myself. I have to
> fight it all the time. In the late sixties, I got so
> wrapped up in environmental causes that a
> good friend, who was an actin' rather than a
> talkin' environmentalist, took me aside and
> told me to get off my damn soap box cause I
> was turnin' everybody off and doin' more harm
> than good. That was damn good advice and I've
> tried to watch myself ever since. We can show
> concern and get the job done for all sorts of
> problems without makin' ourselves and every-
> body else miserable all the time.

The Cimarron Kid has two friends who have taught him much that is included in OZ. They introduced him to Gurdjieff's ideas. Because they spent a year living and working in a Gurdjieff community in New York, they can help illustrate the Kid's point that philosophical systems and ideas tend to make us too serious at times. This is very true of the Gurdjieff work and of many other philosophies and religions. The Kid observed, and his friends agreed, that the time spent at the farm wasn't exactly filled with laughter, frivolity and good times. The Gurdjieff people felt that this is necessary for growth and to work on yourself. The Kid disagrees:

> There is no place in OZ for a joyless attitude or appearance. There **is** a need for quiet and for serious thinkin' and meditation. And, we need to sacrifice and work hard. But, all of this can be done with a smile on your face and in your heart. We don't have to walk around lookin' like death warmed over all the time and infectin' others with our black cloud. I really believe that Gurdjieff didn't want this either and he is being misinterpreted just like some modern day Christians distort the teachings of Christ. Most of the great teachers are probably horrified at what people have done with the ideas and methods they have left us. All the more reason for workin' out your plan for salvation or whatever.

Speaking of Jesus, the Kid feels he was a joyful man and included laughter and festivity in his lifestyle and teachings. The Kid maintains this even though "we get an entirely different picture from a lot of these black-frocked bible-thumpers that rave on about hellfire and damnation." Harvey Cox, the theologian and Christian writer, pointed this out in an article, mentioning the fact that Christ's first miracle was turning water into wine.

Tolkien's Hobbits personify OZ joy when even in their desperate battle against evil they take time out for merry-making. Bilbo Baggins urges all of us at one point to eat more good food and drink good ale and forget our troubles for awhile and that just might make the world a better place.

Tom Robbins, in his book, *Even Cowgirls Get the Blues*, has one of his characters, the Chink, explaining some of the differences between Eastern and Western teachings. He says that Westerners have a great tradition of joy in their religions if you only go back far enough to the hairy, horned, cloven-hoofed gods who loved and laughed and urged their followers to do likewise in celebration of the harvest, fertility or just the great earthy, sensuous world we live in. Too often, seekers in the West throw out the baby with the bathwater in forsaking their own traditions while embracing the Eastern philosophies that more often than not they don't have the resources, background or capabilities to understand and utilize. According to the Chink, we screwed it up in the West, by getting frustrated and up-tight and by distorting and suppressing the old joyful ways under the guise of "divine guidance," usually in some Christian form. We made the old god into Satan and made it a sin to have a good time.

OZ endorses a return to paganism on a limited basis (balance with the other OZ methods and non-interference with our goal-seeking). We want to affirm life rather than deny it. We should revel in the wonders of ourselves and our surroundings, to appreciate and enjoy man, woman and child, plants, animals, air, fire, rocks and water. We need to experience ecstacy and exuberance, to find our peace and happiness and take pleasure in others' good fortune, to love, play and laugh, to be friendly, kind and considerate, to take pride in meeting challenges and in our accomplishments and to celebrate our common needs and fulfillment of these needs. We must be trusting and trustworthy, honest, open and carefree. (Sounds like the Boy Scouts, doesn't it? But, that's all right! In other words, joy in OZ means to maximize the expression of positive emotions.

We can cure ourselves with joy and laughter. This has been shown to be true over and over again. Our health depends so much on our attitude. Even inertia-bound, conservative groups such as the Western medical establishment are beginning to recognize this. Worry, which is a proven killer, is an expression of a negative emotion. If we emphasize positive emotions, our health should improve.

We can improve our health through better nutrition. However, if this is done without joy, as is the case with many popular diets today, then more is probably lost in a total sense than is gained. With the variety of foods available in America and the tremendous amount of nutritional information to which most of us have access, it is easily possible to have our cake and eat it too. Eating should always be a joyful occasion and is often a chance to sharpen other OZ skills as well.

Voltaire, among others, insisted that a primary need of man and a path to happiness is to do work, to "tend our own garden" as it were. Some of this should be hands-on, sweaty, dirty work. The Cimarron Kid likes to haul his own trash and garbage (the part he doesn't recycle) to the city dump. He says it helps keep him aware of this essential duty of keeping our nest clean and it also helps keep him grounded and centered in reality. He says:

> One of the hazards of climbin' the socio-economic ladder is that it separates us from people and tasks that are routine but very important. We forget the necessity of these jobs and how helpful they are to us in findin' out who we are and where we're goin'. We start makin' a livin' instead of makin' a life and we lose a certain lustiness; the vital dance with our environment. Damn, I'm startin' to talk like you, Hudi!

Hard, grubby work, in addition to assisting us with our awareness, simplicity and service, has, to those who are in the know and who haven't forgotten, a wonderful, joyful aspect.

This joy is the same high, the same peak experience, that people involved with fitness and aerobic activities feel when they settle into the sustained rhythm of their exertions. Maybe the absence of physical labor in an increasing number of our lives is responsible for the phenomenal growth in popularity of these interests? In any case, the need for basic physical exertion seems to be fundamental to us all and the more pleasurable these activities the more total benefits we derive from them.

Our intellectual health also requires a steady ration of joy. This may come from humor. It may come from accomplishments such as setting and reaching our goals, solving puzzles or meeting and overcoming challenges. Or, it may derive from playing games or from communication. We all share this need. OZ says we should concentrate on it because it seems to be sadly lacking today. We repeat: WE ARE TOO SERIOUS. A good dose of mental-hedonism is often a valid prescription for the doldrums.

Joy in our relationships is such an obvious need and so easily acquired that it is unnecessary to spend much time on the subject here. The incredible mutual pleasures found through friends, lovers, spouses, our children, our parents, our pets, etc. are to me and to the Kid the source of much love and knowledge. This well of wonders is perpetual, exponential and profound.

According to OZ, we should arrange our homes, yards and clothing so that they also give us joy. We can take pleasure in comfort and simplicity. We can enjoy aesthetic as well as functional values of these parts of our lives. We can also take pride in appearances and in knowing that we don't offend others (a form of aggression). But, the Kid says, "If ya let your ego take charge with your house and your duds and your car and yard, ya get a false joy that'll turn on ya and eat ya up. The worry, time, and expense that your ego demands as its wages for these goodies is OZ-Karma; it'll get ya every time""

Joy at work and at play is also essential. In the workplace, we should keep the smile level high and the frown level low. There are many ways to do this but we can look to the peoples of the Third World civilizations for general examples. On the surface Westerners often see terrible inefficiency and waste in the underdeveloped countries. This usually takes the form of time wastage. Standing in lines, discussing and arguing over the simplest tasks. siestas, laziness and schedules and deliveries that don't make deadlines are a few illustrations. Let's look at this from a different perspective.

Maybe we could learn something from these "primitive societies." What we think is a waste of time may be built-in devices (conscious or unconscious) designed to avoid the rat race. Some of these inefficient activities are the same kinds of things that promote joy. Dancing, singing, loving and playing—being childlike! So what if it takes longer to deliver the mail if people are healthier for it? Many of the debilitating diseases from which we suffer in the industrialized nations can be traced to our hectic pace and stressful work habits. Remember, speed for speed's sake is aggression. If we could learn to reduce the seriousness in our workplace and to tone down the "bigger and faster is better" syndrome, then we might all be happier. Production and quality may suffer some but that would be more than balanced with the increase in joy. And, it would be my guess that, over the long haul, quality of goods and services might instead improve.

When we play games or watch games there should be ample evidence of people having a good time. The same should be said for our hobbies, arts and crafts, and our entertainment. We all know that this isn't always the case. Aggression in the form of competition is usually the culprit. The golfer who breaks his clubs in a fit of anger is a typical cartoon figure. The tennis pro having a temper tantrum for the whole world to see is, sadly, closer to real life than a cartoon. This is also true for certain famous coaches in America who have shown violent and aggressive behavior toward the media, spectators, fellow coaches and even their players and inanimate objects. What beautiful role models for society! We could add to this, stage mothers and little league fathers and the picture gets uglier and uglier. Play is primarily for fun. OZ wants us to get down to basics.

The trick is to achieve all this joyfulness without guilt. This is not easy to do. However, if we include joy as a basic need, right and privilege for everyone and everything in all the ramifications and divisions of our shared existence, then we might feel we are only getting what is due us when we experience pleasure and happiness. OZ demands this.

APPENDIX

Specific Exercises for Working with the Methods of OZ to Improve One's Self in Satisfying One's Goals

The following exercises, activities and practices are taken from the Cimarron Kid's own program. With built-in flexibility for modification, this is what he has done, is doing and will do to work on himself to realize his goals of expanding love and knowledge to whatever degree possible. By his own admission, he is not an OZ master. Since this is his philosophy, however, it seems reasonable to provide the reader who wants to pursue and practice OZ with the Kid's plan of action. It's the only one we have.

Most of these exercises are not original and in fact may seem very obvious and simple. Practicing them together in a harmonious system is rarely done, however. The idea is to spread work on yourself into all areas equally. When you specialize in one or two areas, the athlete who neglects his mind or the intellectual who neglects his body for instance, the costs to you and to all things with which you interact are exorbitant. Specialization can cause accidents. Accidents as well as love and knowledge, exhibit a snowball effect that is persistent and powerful.

The Kid emphasizes that the reader should use these exercises only as a guide to stimulate formation of their own personalized program. For example, any aerobic exercise can be substituted for swimming and walking and any meditative form for Yoga and Tai Chi Chuan. He also stresses that each exercise should involve working simultaneously on multiple parts of OZ and of all parts of your being whenever possible.

Exercises, Practices and Activities

Yoga & Tai Chi Chuan

Both of these exercises are well-suited for OZ because they each incorporate work on many different parts of your being. Yoga helps with flexibility and upper-body strength and endurance as well as the nervous, muscular, circulatory and gastro-intestinal systems. Tai Chi works on balance, lower-body strength and endurance and range of motion. In addition, Tai Chi, which is done very slowly, helps keep the pace of life at a reasonable level. Both activities involve holistic health practices, breathing, meditation and awareness. They also are both simple and nonaggressive. Tai Chi is a martial art, but is used primarily for health and well-being and when it is rarely used for fighting, it is only done in self-defense.

These exercises may be used to draw attention to all parts of your body and environment. By concentrating, breathing and chanting, healing energy is directed to sore, stiff, painful and irritating locations in your being. Work on the reduction of expression of negative emotions may be accomplished through these disciplines. Twenty to thirty minutes a day is attempted on the following:

Yoga—The Sun Exercise (Soorya Namaskar), the Kneeling Pose (Vajrasan), the Lion Pose (Simhasan), the Headstand (Sirshasan), chanting, breathing, meditation and eye, ear, nose and throat exercises and massage (see more complete explanation under sensory exercises below).

Tai Chi—The solo exercise, long form, Yang style (as taught by Master Chu Fang Chu and Steve Chatfield), balance, meditation, breathing and leg-strength exercises.

There are many excellent sources of information concerning Yoga and Tai Chi. However, it is best to take courses in them and enlist the aid of teachers so as to learn them properly andin the right context and perspective.

Sensory Exercises

These practices may be used as part of a regular meditative routine to strengthen and sharpen the senses:

1. Incense is burned to give a focus for the sense of smell and to add a little pleasure to this time of day.
2. Music is played to sharpen hearing, provide rhythm and for its relaxing and pleasurable qualities.
3. Eyes are rotated, focused and un-focused in rhythm with the music.

4. Breathing and chanting exercises are performed in time with the music and in coordination with abdominal and intestinal muscle contractions.

5. Prior to or during exercises, a small amount of refreshing, healthful beverage such as honey and vinegar in warm water, Aloe Vera juice or other fruit juices or coffee or tea may be consumed with attention drawn to the sense of taste and the gastrointestinal tract.

6. When the head and face are infused with blood and oxygen after practicing the Headstand, the head, face, eyes, ears, nose and throat are massaged and the tongue and throat are exercised by the Lion Pose.

7. The sense of touch is under constant scrutiny with awareness of balance and in contact with the exercise surfaces and with the temperature, humidity and pressure of the air.

In addition to the above, participation in the activities below are advised on an irregular basis. They are all attempts at looking at, listening to, tasting, touching and smelling things differently

1. Lay on your stomach in the grass and look long and hard at the micro-world that exists there— the insects and other organic life, the rocks, minerals and soil. Pursue this with a magnifying glass.

2. Look at the sky with a telescope or binoculars.

3. Go into a strange place, shut your eyes and just listen for five minutes.

4. Do the same as number three but in a familiar place.

5. Find invisible things and then figure out how to draw pictures of them.

6. Occasionally, make eating a brand new experience and adventure by cooking and tasting exotic and foreign foods and beverages. (The Kid once ate a pack rat while participating in a survival test. He said it tasted like rabbit.)

7. See how long you can go during a normal day without talking, seeing or hearing.

8. Get together with friends and try to identify a variety of common and uncommon objects by the sense of touch alone—a great ice-breaker game.

9. Make love without touching.

Aerobic Exercises

Both Yoga and Tai Chi are touted as complete fitness disciplines, but the Kid feels that, for his needs, they don't work on the cardiovascular system enough. Therefore, he includes some kind of aerobic activity in his program a minimum of three times a week for at least 20 minutes each time. Currently, he is concentrating on swimming and walking but has at various times used running, bicycling, hiking and cross-country skiing for this purpose. Anything that suits your needs and abilities is fine but the best research shows that people, to be fit, need to get their pulse rate up to a certain level and sustain it at that level no less than three times per week for twenty to twenty-five minutes each time. To determine your target pulse rate, take 220 minus your age multiplied by 0.75. Using the Kid as an example, 220 - 45 = 175, 175 x 0.75 = 131. The Kid tries to keep his pulse in that vicinity when he is doing these exercises.

Whatever your own program entails you should never begin any strenuous exercise without first preparing yourself by doing a variety of stretching, bending and twisting exercises. The Kid often uses the Yoga and Tai Chi for this but adds some strength and endurance exercises such as sit-ups and push-ups.

Oftentimes, but not on a systematic schedule, the Cimarron Kid throws in an extended, aerobic activity just for fun. These are usually family and/or friend oriented and take place on weekends or vacations. Experiences like hiking, peak climbing, cross-country or downhill skiing and bicycling fit in here. Even though the primary reason for these experiences is pure enjoyment, there is the bonus of additional aerobics.

The Kid realizes he is sort of a fanatic about outdoor, physical activity and correspondingly makes sure that he keeps things in balance. He says he averages about an hour a day on these things and this is more than is necessary for good health. He achieves a lot of joy from these, however, and experiences togetherness with family and friends, so for him it satisfies his needs. He also states that his program is in constant evolution, having just recently switched from fifteen years of jogging to swimming and walking. From the OZ standpoint, walking is probably the best aerobic activity because it is simple, nonaggressive and allows the participant to be aware of many things. The Kid believes he'll probably end up using walking entirely for his aerobic needs but for right now it is too time-consuming and he still isn't far enough advanced in OZ to let go of his Tarzan imitation. (Use of upper body exercises while walking, such as the new Heavy Hands program, can increase the pulse rate and thus reduce the time commitment to walking while also giving the arms, chest, shoulders and back flexibility, strength and endurance training.)

There are many aerobic activities to choose from but whatever you do should be joyful and should work on many things at once. All aerobic exercises can be used to sharpen meditation and awareness skills. The Kid often chants in rhythm with them or focuses his attention on different parts of his body to observe their function and interaction with his environment. He tries to be aware of sounds, color, movement, odors, etc. as he walks and swims.

Nutritional Practices

Be aware of **your** needs. Be aware of harmful foods and practices both in a qualitative and quantitative sense. Be aware of caloric intake and expenditure. Expand your knowledge and love (self love) here. Be simple and nonaggressive, but have fun! The Cimarron Kid says:

> I purty much eat and drink what I want. I just
> try to follow these simple rules. Eat arid drink
> slowly and lightly when possible. Increase
> simple, useful, natural foods and beverages
> and reduce the amount of artificial, prepared
> and harmful foods. But, I sure intend to enjoy

life too. I try to not make a religion out of it and not to worry if I scarf down some junk food now and then. Ya gotta have variety and joy.

Specific Dietary Instructions that fit with OZ but shouldn't tie anyone down too much:

1. Increase the amount of high-fiber foods in your diet.
2. Decrease the amount of fat in your diet.
3. Limit consumption of salt, sugar, caffeine and alcohol to reasonable levels.
4. Be moderate. (The Kid has always had trouble with this one but everyone from Aristotle to Jimmy Carter has praised the virtue of moderation. It is still good advice to say, "Nothing in excess, everything in moderation." Remember the statement, "Too much sex is almost enough"? That observation of human behavior, with the change of one word, could apply here and many other places as well.)

The Stop Exercise

This is an awareness exercise that the Kid learned from his study of Gurdjieff. Whatever you are doing, you can use this exercise to help make you sharply aware of imperfections in your procedure. This consists of consciously stopping abruptly any physical, emotional or intellectual actions and directing your attention at what your various parts are doing. Possibly, the effects of your actions on yourself or on anything else are not those that are desired and unawareness has shielded you from this knowledge. Stop yourself at irregular and infrequent times in all facets of your life and observe what is happening. You will be surprised. Here are some situations where the stop exercise might be applied:

1. During physical exercise or the playing of games or sports, stop yourself when you can and check balance, muscle tension, your emotions, your breathing and heart rate, your fitness level, etc. Maybe muscles are unnecessarily tensed and can be relaxed or possibly anger is running away with you. Joy could be absent and you might be punishing yourself to dangerous extremes.

2. Stop yourself during arguments and listen intently to what the other person is saying. Then think about what you have been doing and saying. Think about all parts of your being and their actions. The quiet won't hurt anything and may stop or slow down a fruitless encounter.

3. Stop yourself at work, at your job or on hobbies or crafts. What are your goals and are your activities leading you toward or away from them? Are you out of balance with your emotions or is your intellect trying to control everything? How can you get more joy or efficiency into your work? How can you manage time better or reduce the stress in your workplace? Pay attention to

the smallest things and sometimes this will give you the answers you seek.

4. While you are involved in entertainment, recreation or sex, mentally yell stop at your emotions or thoughts and analyze and evaluate what's going on.

All this may sound ridiculous and it might seem that it would interfere with our functioning as a normal human being. However, it can be done in an unobtrusive manner and need not take more than a few seconds to accomplish. Most of us go through life asleep or partly asleep so the time spent on the stop exercise will not exact noticeable changes in our outward appearance or behavior. What it will do, if practiced properly, is to make profound changes in our overall behavior over a long period of time. It is essential, in the practice of OZ, to include some kind of analytical and evaluative practice such as this in our total package so that we can assess our participation with each method of OZ and the balance between the methods.

Something that helps considerably with the stop exercise, and with many of the other exercises as well, is to include others in the activity. Specifically here, this would mean to have someone else tell us to "stop" at varied and different times.

Self-Remembering Exercises

This was also taken from Gurdjieff studies. The Kid learned these from teachers and friends who have studied at various schools based on the teachings of Gurdjieff and Ouspensky. Self-remembering can be thought of here as being synonymous with awareness in the OZ system. It simply means to remember yourself at times when we are most likely to be unaware. Included here are some of the practices the Kid uses to work on awareness:

1. Remember the first bite you take at each meal. Not after the fact, but actually while you chomp down.

2. Remember yourself when you walk through doorways.

3. Remember yourself by purposely disrupting and breaking habitual behavior. Do something backward, in an opposite or inverse fashion, slower than normal, faster than normal, with the wrong hand, etc. Wash dishes with your left hand rather than your right. Mow the lawn in circles instead of at right angles. Walk to work or to the grocery store instead of driving. Exchange roles with your spouse, child, parent, friend or a stranger. Stay up at night and sleep during the day. (The Kid's Tai Chi teacher once told him to stand in front of a shelf which is at eye-level and lift something off the shelf but to take five minutes to do this rather than the normal two seconds. "It sounds weird, but I learned a lot from that little trick," said the Kid.)

For these self-remembering exercises, choose mundane, everyday, recurring events. The kinds that you do without thought. Nobody thinks about the first bite they eat at each meal or when they walk through doors. It is surprising how difficult this is to do. This will at the very least show us how often we are asleep and not paying attention.

Culling

In the interests of OZ simplicity and awareness, it is a good idea to periodically survey our material goods and cull out those things that are not used or that cause us worry or hassle. Here are some things the Cimarron Kid has worked on in this category:

1. **Books**—It was the Kid's practice, in his earlier years, to buy, shelve and display books of all size, shape, content and description. He frequented garage sales and auctions and looked through mail order catalogues and book stores and amassed quite an array of reading material. After enlightening himself as to the role his ego played in all this and what a small fraction of the books were actually read or used as resources, he decided to and did reduce his library to the essentials—about one-tenth its prior size.

2. **Phonograph Records**—The identical process, as with books, was followed with his record collection. "I had so damn many records," said the Kid, "that I never really listened to my favorites. And, I was always fussin' over 'em, arrangin', storin', and catalogin' til they ate up so much time some-

thin' had to give. They did! I gave about two-thirds of 'em away."

3. **Other Collection**—This was also applied to guns, musical instruments and rock and fossil collections. "And, I'm just gettin' started," says the Kid.

Don't limit yourself to material possessions, however. Culling can be practiced on emotional, intellectual and spiritual baggage. On sports, hobbies, recreation, entertainment, work, obligations, duties, social schedules, friends, children, lovers, wives, husbands, ... But, watch out! Obsession with anything, including culling, causes imbalance and that's an Oklahoma Zen No! No! Moderation should be practiced here also.

Siddhartha, in Herman Hesse's book by that title, ended up with practically nothing after trying just about everything. By his own choice, he reduced his life and work to ferrying people, in a primitive fashion, across a river. Here, he required little and seemed to be content and fulfilled to perform this small service and to commune with nature. But, he was an uncommon man, operating on a different plane from most of us.

Culling leads right into ...

Giving

It helps us work on all aspects of OZ when we give. This refers to any kind of giving, material or otherwise. And, it certainly includes, but is not limited to, organized giving such as Christmas and birthday gifts, United Way fund drives and volunteer work. This necessarily involves planned as well as spontaneous giving that is meant to benefit the giver as well as the receiver. What is meant by this, is that we should be consciously and purposefully aware of our greedy, graspy ways and force ourselves to give things away to counter these negative emotions. This is obviously an OZ benefit. A few examples will help explain this:

1. A friend or even a stranger is admiring something we possess and we just, wham"bam, say, "Take it. It's yours." This sounds crazy in today's assertive and possessive world but to experience it promotes joy, simplicity, nonaggression, growth, service and awareness.

2. We have become accomplished at some art and a novice asks us to give a lesson or some pointers on improving their abilities and skills. Even though we may not think we have the time, patience or resources, we should give freely but always keep in mind the need for balance in our own life.

3. We are thinking about having a garage, patio or yard sale. Many people are doing this these days. Instead, we could give all the stuff to a charity or whoever we think might want or need it. We could even be more rebellious against current trends and not deduct it from our income taxes thereby extending our giving to the government as well. A healthy disdain for money and profit-maximizing is helpful to OZ development.

4. A stranger is standing by a coin-operated stamp machine, car wash or wherever without the correct change. If we recognize their plight, and if we are aware, then we could give them what they need and do it with a smile.

Keep in mind that these are not entirely unselfish acts. The benefits that we and the rest of society, in a Big Brain as well as a normal communicative sense, derive from giving far outweigh our costs. However, and this is a subtle but important point, give too much and you're out of balance. We must be aware of our own needs and limits or giving can be transformed into taking.

Humor Exercises

We should include a reasonable amount of humor in all facets of our lives. This must be natural. It can't be forced. We must realize that it can be irritating to everyone concerned if this behavior is extreme, ill-timed or out of place. Being aware of these limitations, the Kid believes it is an act of love when we:

1. Tease each other at work or play.
2. Play tricks and practical jokes.
3. Tell jokes and stories and put a lot of energy, creativity and action into the telling.
4. Entertain.
5. Act in an off-the-wall, outrageous, bizarre fashion.
6. Make puns and spoonerisms of normal

conversation.

7. Seek out comedy and humor in all situations.

8. Learn to laugh at ourselves and not be threatened by humor.

We can't emphasize enough the importance of being aware of the limits contained in this exercise. It can turn sour very quickly if we are not cognizant of these limitations. With the best intentions, we may, at the least be a bore or at the worst, aggressive and cruel. We should also be aware of our motivations. We should be of service to ourselves and others in the interest of joy and not be acting the clown simply to enhance our own image and our popularity.

Emotional Exercises

Be aware of the expression of negative emotions in your life and attempt to reduce them by:

1. Pick some negative emotion, greed for example, and observe yourself and others over a period of time to determine its impact.

2. Choose a positive emotion which opposes your choice in number one. In this example, generosity would oppose greed. Express it inwardly and outwardly in an attempt to overcome the expression of negativity.

3. Repeat numbers one and two as needed.

Intellectual Exercises

Study what your mind is doing in a normal day. If not exercised enough, challenge your mind with the following:

1. Puzzles, games and problems to solve.
2. Take a course through a free school, continuing education or through some other channel.
3. Learn new skills, hobbies, crafts and arts, or perfect old ones.
4. Turn off the television set and do something else for a week or a month.
5. Quit doing other things and watch television for twenty-four hours straight.
6. Look on adversity as a challenge and a teacher. Force yourself to read something you have always hated—history for instance. When you find yourself in unpleasant social situations or weather, don't cuss your luck but rather think how you can turn things to your advantage to help you reach your goals. Learn from these conditions or force yourself to find joy in them.
7. Develop and write your own philosophy.
8. Identify all the weeds in your yard by their scientific names and learn to love them for their beauty and function.
9. Work on allowing your intuition to coexist and have equal time with your intellect.

Nonaggression Exercises

1. Learn to play the New Games. These are becoming more popular and can be learned from books, recreational services and centers, school counselors and enlightened physical education teachers. They consist of games that are played primarily for fun (competition is practically nonexistent), that maximize participation and safety and minimize ego involvement and organization.

2. Learn to play old games with New Games' rules: play hard, play fair, have fun, everybody wins and nobody gets hurt.

3. Isolate areas of competition in your life and try to reduce them.

4. Determine situations where cooperation seems to be the primary operant and learn to capitalize on this and to apply it elsewhere.

5. Find practices and times of self-abuse and learn to reduce or stop them. Try to balance emotional needs with health needs.

6. The next time you find a spider in your house or a snake in your yard or path, don't kill it. Walk around it, avoid it, learn to live with it or remove it gently to another place.

7. The next time you feel the urge to scratch your initials on a tree, rock or a National Park sign, don't.

8. Don't litter.

9. Consume less, produce less and recycle.

10. Reduce your participation in activities that pollute or over-populate the earth.

11. Do what you can to help reduce the danger of nuclear holocaust.

12. Don't waste.

13. When you feel aggressive or if someone is treating you in an aggressive manner, concentrate on your own personal prayer, mantra or the image of something reassuring and/or comforting. The OZ prayer, "Everything in the Universe is sacred and deserves our tender, loving care" works well for the Kid. So does the image of a calm body of water with swans floating gracefully thereon. You know what would work for you, so use it if you care to.

14. A physical corollary to number thirteen is to consciously relax your face and stomach muscles when threatened. It is surprising how this little effort can dilute a potentially explosive situation.

15. Practice nonaggression exercises to help strengthen other skills and use other skills to help reduce aggression. BALANCE! ONE-NESS OF THE COSMOS! CIRCLE, CONTI-NUITY, EQUILIBRIUM!

17. Kiss a rock. The Irish do it all the time.

18. Kiss a beaver.

Everything has to be considered in context. When OZ says, "Don't kill spiders or snakes" it means that this practice will help you be aware of aggression and violence. It doesn't mean that it is wrong to kill—there is no implied morality here. If a spider or anything else threatenes your peace and happiness, then by all means do what you have to do to take care of the situation. Sometimes we have to go to extremes to learn lessons but once learned we can back off to a more moderate position.

Service Exercise

Try to be a better listener. This in itself is a full-time job.

Exercise to Promote Joy

Be childlike, not childish.

— Nuff Said! —

ANOTHER NOTE FROM THE KID

After readin' the rough draft of this book I decided I just couldn't let it go without addin' my two-cents worth at the end. I think Hudi did a purty good job of presentin' OZ, but I'm concerned about false impressions readers might get from the book.

First, I don't want anybody to think that I'm some kind of a guru or somethin'. Hudi pointed out a lot of my faults and he hit the nail right on the head most of the time. One thing he didn't mention enough is that just because I invented this here philosophy doesn't mean I'm an expert at it. I try to live by it but many times I fail. Some of the things I haven't even tried myself, I've only thought about 'em. And, a lot of things may prove worthless so I'll throw 'em out and find something else. I'm sure that the next time I read this I'll find a bunch of stuff that needs changin'.

Second, there's nobody that can be perfect in practicin' OZ. It's set up on purpose that way. It's like Tai Chi, which even the masters, after practicin' for forty or fifty years, still make mistakes at. Each method is hard enough to work on by itself, especially awareness, but when ya start to harmonize everything, that's when it really hits the fan. Just thought ya needed some extra warnin'.

Third, I don't harbor any "delusions of grandeur" about this book. I know that there probably ain't a half dozen people that will agree with it and there's a good chance that not many more will even read the damn thing—especially all the way through. But, that's all right. It had to be done and here it is. Maybe it will be of some service, if just to get folks stirred up a little.

The Kid

And last, here's a little song I just now made up to the tune of *Darlin' Cory* (or, for you bluegrassers, *Lil.' Maggie*):

I Don't Want To Be Your Guru
The Cimarron Kid (1983)

I don't want to be your guru,
I don't want to be a saint.
I just want to be myself boys,
A hero I damn sure ain't.

I'd really like to be your gadfly,
I'd sure like to tickle your mind.
I hope I'm some help to ya brother,
Your peace and happiness to find.

Let's don't play "Consciousness-A-Go-Go,"
Let's just spin the wheel of life.
I don't want to be your daddy,
And, I really don't care to be your wife.

I know and love myself better,
I know and love the world better too,
Since writin' this book for ya sister,
I hope it does somethin' for you.

I don't want to be your guru,
A preacher is the last thing I want to be.
So, take this book my friend or leave it,
Either way is all the same to me.

I do take pride in what I've done here,
Just like the others who heard the call.
But, it's just a small part of the game girls,
I don't want to be a guru at all.

I don't want to be your guru,
A friend is what I really want to be.
We're ridin' this wheel together, pilgrim.
Spur it one more time for me.

Yeehaw, Yawhoo!

Cimarron Kid

Sometimes known as Grizzly,
Sometimes known as Silvertip,
And long ago known as a
Bloody Bastard from Smokey Hill

P.S. Here's a little Oklahoma Zen Guitar instrumental I wrote in 1966. It seems appropriate to add it at this point.

Variations on the Maggie Theme,

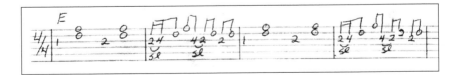

Appendix

The Cimarron Kid (1966)
Variations I through Variation V
(S1 = slide, CH = choke, H = hammer-on, P = pull-off)

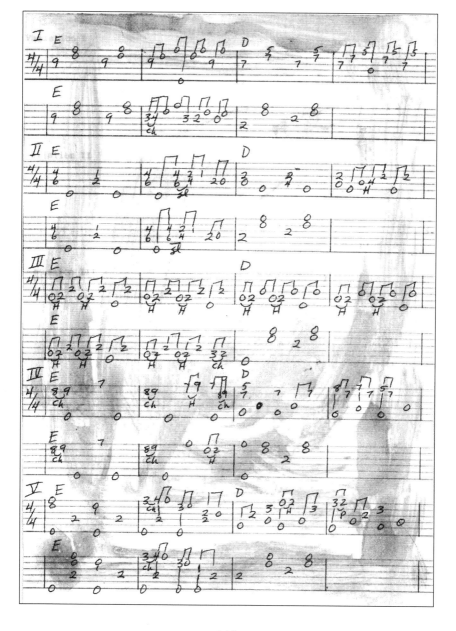

ABOUT THE AUTHOR

Roger Hudiburg is a retired science teacher, a musician, an artist and a sometime vagabond. He wrote his book for his family and friends who were often wondering what he was all about. He also wanted to share his art and his musical compositions with his readers.

Made in the USA
San Bernardino, CA
25 October 2013